IF YOU READ ME, ROCK THE TOWER!

Bob Stevens

AERO
A division of TAB BOOKS Inc.
Blue Ridge Summit, PA 17214

FIRST EDITION

THIRD PRINTING

Printed and published in the United States of America by Aero, a division of
TAB BOOKS Inc.

Library of Congress Cataloging in Publication Data

Stevens, Bob, 1923-
   If you read me— rock the tower.

   1. American wit and humor, Pictorial.   2. Caricatures
and cartoons—United States.   I. Title.
      NC1429.S64A4   1987   741.5'973   87-1854
            ISBN 0-8306-8650-9 (pbk.)

Foreword

Remember the old line about "They laughed when I sat down to play the piano . . ."? Well, when Bob Stevens sits down to "play" his drawing board "piano," he's the one doing the laughing. Bob's cartoon ideas so tickle his highly honed sense of humor that they're all thoroughly laugh-tested by the time they appear on paper. Perhaps that's his key to success as a cartoonist—he's able to see humor in a situation where others might not.

For instance, there was one of his "Stop Squawk!" items that shows a twin engine plane with a pilot sweating out a suddenly dead engine. He asks the tower to clear the runway; the tower asks his position. The pilot replies: "I'm executive vice president of the first national bank. Please expedite!"

Shortly after that appeared in PRIVATE PILOT, we had several bankers call to request enlarged copies for display on their walls; they thought it was hilariously funny. Now, anytime you can get a banker to laugh, you've really struck a funnybone.

Bob Stevens is all funnybones when it comes to aviation. His long experience in both military and civilian flying enables him to see the lighter sides of both, even though he's a thorough-going professional when it comes to flying his own airplane. Conversations with other pilots, chatter with tower or approach controllers, all register potential ideas for his future cartoons. Some of the ludicrous events he portrays even have happened to him—he's usually the guy with the baseball cap and Smilin' Jack mustache.

A conversation with Bob on the subject of his next submission always turns into a half-hour laugh session. His explanations of plot or theme are interspersed with chuckles so that when he's finished, you're both laughing away at the subject. Funny thing is (pun intended), his cartoons always turn out better than he describes them. Funnier, more ridiculous, more expressive.

And that's another thing. Stevens seems able to get more expression out of a squiggly penned line than many artists get from an entire oil painting. Look at his people, his planes; their expressions are pure interpretive art.

A sure sign of Bob Stevens' wide acceptance is the frequency with which one sees his cartoon art posted on flight operations bulletin, boards. These might be related to the poster art of modern China; if one wants to make a social comment, one tacks up a poster (or clipping) that best expresses one's feelings. One bulletin board we saw had five " . . .Squawks!" pinned up!

I have this picture of Bob that comes to mind whenever I think of him. He's there in his avocado tree-shaded studio, surrounded by stacks of magazines and artist's paraphernalia, and he's laughing . . . he's just come up with some more cartoon ideas . . . and I can hear the laughter across the miles.

Dennis Shatttuck
Editor, Private Pilot

AUTHOR'S NOTES AND ACKNOWLEDGEMENTS

I'm really a story teller with a brush and pen. As anyone who's ever hung around an airport and done some hangar flying knows, pilots and ground crewmen are full of stories. The pilots' lounge, airport greasy spoon cafe, tool crib area, control tower—anywhere people gather who are hooked on the sky— are perfect breeding grounds for the cartoon stories appearing in this book.

I've been listening to, and recording, these stories for almost four decades . . . ever since my first solo in a 65 hp Interstate Cadet, circa 1941. I merely stage a funny story graphically— much the way a movie director sets the scene for a "take." It's fun and not a bit like work at all. One of my pleasures has been meeting the many genuinely fine folks who people the sky.

As to acknowledgments, I want to thank most sincerely the editors of *Air Force* and *Private Pilot* for permission to reprint these cartoons which first appeared in their publications. *Air Force* launched my professional military cartooning career and *Private Pilot* followed suit on the civilian side.

A great number of friends, acquaintances and a bunch of total strangers have contributed ideas for the cartoons in this book. I counted to about 40 contributors before deciding it would be a poor idea to list all of them by name. Usually the story, or gag, is a hand-me-down and I'd be bound to omit someone in the chain . . . or worse, the originator himself. There *are* a few contributors that require singling out because of the sheer volume of really funny stuff they've provided. These are: the Confederate Air Force, Harlingen, Texas; the U. S. Air Force Academy "Talon" newspaper and its staff of cadets in Colorado Springs; Mr. Martin Leeuwis of the Royal Netherlands Air Force; and Mr. Paul Dean, feature writer for the Los Angeles Times— whose prose adorns a part of this book. To these folks, and all the others not mentioned, I extend my heart-filled thanks for sharing their humor with an audience I know will appreciate it.

Bob Stevens
Fallbrook
January 1980

DEDICATION

To Barb, wife, friend, critic, copyreader—
and the best damn co-pilot in my world.

PART I

In this section—the first half of the book—we deal with general aviation. Being an old military troop, I always thought General Aviation was a rank held by no less than a two star. I came to learn later in my flying experience that "general" refers to a catch-all category in aviation which includes everything that is not military or air carrier. More than 98% of *all* civil aviation activity within the U. S. falls into general aviation's ranks.

Most of the humor in aviation involves communications or the lack thereof. The reader will find this theme running through both parts of the book. Note: If pure military aviation humor is your thing, go directly to Part II (page 75). We warn you, though, you'll be missing a lot of laughs. For aviation humor is pretty universal. What's funny to an antiquer or home-built aficionado will also break up 747 or Starfighter driver.

Besides *communications,* in Part I we'll cover *training, maintenance* and *the buying and selling of things aeronautical.* (I don't think there's a bigger patsy in the world for a new gimmick—be it a computer, clipboard, headset, or new way of computing fuel remaining—than a pilot.)

Finally, we'll wind up Part I with *Pot Pourri.* This section of the book defies categorization. You'll find a little bit about air shows and fly-ins (which is becoming harder to do with escalating fuel costs). We close the section with a few regulations spawned eons ago in the 1920s entitled "Concerning the Operation of Aircraft."

The deathless prose appearing on the opposite page entitled "Why I Want to be a Pilot" is attributed to a student of Jefferson School, Beaufort, S.C., and was first published in the South Carolina Aviation News. It epitomizes the aviation world as seen through the eyes of an eight year old. I think it's a classic.

It is interesting to note that when I first drew this cartoon, I reversed several of the letters "R" to dramatize the fact that it was written by a youthful author. This brought a storm of protest from professional educators. People pointed out that, "only Monogoloid idiots reverse their R's," etc., etc. It became apparent to me that a few people read aviation humor just like they read political cartoons, e.g. they're always looking for flaws that offend their professional domain—then they stick it to the artist. In the trade, cartoonists call these people, "wheel counters." So far, I've been relatively lucky in this respect. I've had letters regarding the captions I've put on cartoons, but rarely will anyone criticize the number of engines, the number of wings and the general configuration of the airplanes I draw.

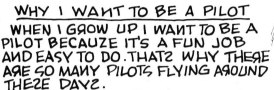

WHY I WANT TO BE A PILOT

WHEN I GROW UP I WANT TO BE A PILOT BECAUZE IT'S A FUN JOB AND EASY TO DO. THATS WHY THERE ARE SO MANY PILOTS FLYING AROUND THEZE DAYS.

PILOTS DONT NEED MUCH SCHOOL. THEY JUST HAVE TO LEARN TO READ NUMBERS SO THEY CAN READ THEIR INSTRUMENTS.

I GUESS THEY SHOULD BE ABLE TO READ A ROAD MAP, TOO...

PILOTS SHOULD BE BRAVE SO THEY WONT GET SCARED IF IT'S FOGGY AND THEY CAN'T SEE, OR IF A WING OR MOTOR FALLS OFF...

PILOTS HAVE TO HAVE GOOD EYES TO SEE THROUGH THE CLOUDS, AND THEY CANT BE AFRAID OF THUNDER OR LIGHTENING BECAUZE THEY ARE MUCH CLOSER TO THEM THAN WE ARE.

THE SALARY PILOTS MAKE IS ANOTHER THING I LIKE. THEY MAKE MORE MONEY THAN THEY KNOW WHAT TO DO WITH. THIS IS BECAUZE MOST PEOPLE THINK THAT FLYING A PLANE IS DANGEROUS, EXCEPT PILOTS DON'T BECAUZE THEY KNOW HOW EASY IT IS.

I HOPE I DONT GET AIR-SICK BE-CAUZE I GET CAR-SICK AND IF I GET AIR-SICK I COULDN'T BE A PILOT AND THEN I WOULD HAVE TO GO TO WORK.

Just suppose that the FAA had sprung into existence the instant the bureaucrats heard about "those fellows down there at Kitty Hawk with a flying machine." I'm trying very hard to keep this book apolitical, but I can't help commenting on the FAA and some of the bureaucratic machinations that pilots have to go through to (a) get a license, (b) fly and maintain an airplane, and (c) sell it when they're finished with it. In any event, the aircraft depicted is an exact replica of the Wright flyer. I obtained the original 3-view plans from the patent office in Washington, D.C. I wanted to be extremely careful that I did not draw any fire from aviation historians . . . this airplane is almost a holy shrine.

As in the case of many of the pages to follow, there is not a continuity of ideas. Perhaps I'll have a single "gag" cartoon, a panel and wind it up with a strip which will develop a story line. The panel entitled *Aviation Glossary* was taken from a Confederate AF booklet published back in the '60s. You'll find these little gems scattered throughout the book. CAF troops put in a lot of work rebuilding WWII aircraft, but they also have a pretty good time partying. They'll gather in the Confederate Air Force bar after a hard day's work and put together some very funny material. The aviation glossary was one of their efforts. I want to recognize one man in particular, Lloyd Nolan of the CAF. His wit and humor has long permeated the official "dispatches" that are issued by the Confederate Air Force Headquarters to the troops in the field.

WESTERN ONION 17 Dec 1903
To: Wright Bros:
  Unable to approve standard seaweed departure account traffic - cross the 315 radial of shellfish VOR at flight level zero zero five - contact oyster departure control on 127.3, if unable try and hold 2 mi east of Sandbar, right hand turns inbound.. expect..

and I SAY TO HELL WITH IT! LET'S PUT 'ER BACK IN THE SHED!

HOW TO WIN FRIENDS and INFLUENCE PILOTS - ESPECIALLY IN CONGESTED AREAS...

(UNICOM)

PULL UP! THERE'S AN AIRCRAFT BELOW YOU!!

and SO ON ACROSS 4 COUNTIES

AVIATION GLOSSARY

SLOW FLIGHT: ONE THAT LASTS BEYOND THE BLADDER LIMITS.

(CLOSEUP OF EYEBALLS)

This cartoon is entitled "Chicken in the Sky." We deal with the innermost thoughts of man—a pretty terrifying subject. Wordsworth pegged it with, "voyaging through strange seas of thought, alone." Those of you who are pilots will no doubt remember your first solo cross country. Those thoughts we harbored and worried about prior to and during the flight will long be cherished and remembered, won't they?

It seems the worst possible situation can always be dreamed up in a neophyte's mind. One scene in this particular sequence covers the computation of how much fuel you consumed for a given leg or distance. "Fuel figurin' " takes about all of the time a trainee has between check points when he isn't looking out the window trying to recognize something. Fuel is pretty important to an airplane. Engine failure occurs when the fuel tanks become filled by air. Then there's a very definite force that acts upon the bird when the engine stops—gravity. To accommodate this, you must go down. This fundamental aerodynamic principle occupies much of your thought in an aircraft low on fuel.

Flying has been described as "hours and hours of boredom—interspersed with moments of stark terror." Back on the ground, ol' Hotshot will pass off the most harrowing of mental trips as "routine."

"CHICKEN IN THE SKY"

Training is training, land or water. Over-concentration has caused many a mishap. In this particular case, the pilot getting checked out on floats has forgotten which kind of firma he's going to land on. (Landing a sea plane on the gound is filled with terror—that's what the words "terror firma" comes from.)

Over-concentration results from, in many cases, being over conditioned. We hear horns and see lights or indicators to tell us of certain conditions in the aircraft. To illustrate: A friend of mine was all set up to land and then was sent around. He pulled his gear up, made his go-around, came back in and forgot to lower the gear the second time. When asked later by the accident board why he didn't hear the repeated warnings of the tower that his gear was up, he said he couldn't hear the tower because of that loud warning horn blowing in his ear.

This story was told to me by Dick Rossi, a friend and neighbor who was one of the original fighter pilots in the Flying Tigers. Dick was in the first group to join General Chennault in China before the United States entered WWII. An easy-going type, but a terror in a P-40, he became an ace before the U. S. entered war, and finished his flying career as a DC-8 Captain with the Flying Tiger line. Dick took his flight training with the Navy and swears this story actually happened at Pensacola.

TRANSITIONING FROM LAND TYPE BIRDS TO FLOAT PLANES — *and* VICE VERSA — CAN BE FRAUGHT WITH PERIL...

PULL UP, BILL!

OHMYGOSH! THAT WAS CLOSE!! I FORGOT WE WERE ON FLOATS!

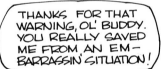

THE NEXT APPROACH IS MADE OVER THE PROPER ELEMENT...

NOW, *THAT'S* MORE LIKE IT!

THANKS FOR THAT WARNING, OL' BUDDY. YOU REALLY SAVED ME FROM AN EM-BARRASSIN' SITUATION!

We present herewith a view of a trainer from the right seat. A subtitle might be, "Why Instructors Get Gray." If you've ever *had to* instruct, and I use the words *had to* because I don't think anyone ever really volunteers to instruct, unless you're desperate to build up flying time. I instructed after WWII and found it to be a most harrowing experience.

It's difficult to describe flight instruction; you try to cover as much as you can on the ground with the student. However, most of the nitty-gritty is accomplished in the air with arm waving, flapping of hands and screaming at the top of your lungs over the engine noise. At least that's the way it was in the early days. Nowadays, more sophisticated intercom systems are provided for communications and you can transmit, "Get your head out of your_____" more emphatically than in the past. But, basically, it's still a matter of trying to pound into a student's head those things which were pounded into your own . . . and survive.

THE VIEW FROM THE RIGHT SEAT
(OR, WHY INSTRUCTORS GET GREY)

"OKAY BUNIONHEAD, DON'T YOU THINK IT'S ABOUT TIME YOU STARTED YOUR FLARE?"

"WELL, YAS, I'D SAY WE'RE OVERSHOOTING OUR FINAL JUST A TAD"

"WE'RE GOING TO NEED A LITTLE WORK ON OUR CROSS-WIND APPROACH TECHNIQUE, *AREN'T* WE?"

"FER STARTERS, YOU *MIGHT* ASK THE TOWER WHAT'S THE ACTIVE!"

Although the bird in this particular sequence is a military T-6, it could have just as well been any general aviation aircraft with tandem seats. With this seating arrangement, you're at a distinct disadvantage because sitting behind the student pilot you are unable to slug 'im. You must depend upon leather lungs or a Gosport, which is a talking tube. As we pointed out earlier, communications is aviation humor's strong suit. The lack of communications was not *always* due to equipment malfunction. In this particular case, there was a short circuit between the student's ears.

There's one thing that will always get a student's attention— rap his knees by shaking the stick (in aircraft so equipped) or yell at him. I once had a student "freeze" on the stick (I thought this only happened in old movies). He had a pathological fear of stalls. So we stalled, he pulled back on the stick and we promptly entered a beautiful tight spin. I was unable to wrest the controls away from him. After several shoves at the stick and a couple of verbal commands, I cupped my hands around his ear and screamed at the top of my lungs, "Let Go!" He dang near jumped out of his skin and immediately took his hand off the stick. To say I was able to recover is redundant—I'm writing this book. This type of communication is very effective.

and OUR NEOPHYTE DUTIFULLY RESPONDS...

17

This cartoon was drawn especially for instrument pilots or instrument trainees. Most pilots are prone to "flight checkitis," a condition aggravated by being under the hood on an instrument flight check. Here we have a bird's eye view of such a ride.

Under the hood, the trainee's sweat flows in direct proportion to the amount of diabolical schemes the instructor can dream up. For example, he can always start you into a right hand turn and then subtly reverse the turn. Your inner ear thinks you're still turning to the right and all the instruments appear to be telling you outrageous lies. Or, he can pull the airplane up into a near stall, roll it on its side and say, "Okay, it's all yours." When you look at all the dancing needles and the horizon line is vertical, it's very difficult to differentiate up from down.

Suffice to say, under the hood is blacker than the inside of a cow. If not under the hood, you're wearing a set of blinders like ol' Dobbin, which blocks out all vision except for about a square foot of the panel. Vertigo, or as the FAA likes to call it, "spacial disorientation," can be described as feeling your stomach going one way, the seat of your pants another, and your brain still a third direction. There's another sure indication you're getting into trouble under the hood—sweat from your palms begins dripping off the top of the wheel. On top of all these sadistic maneuvers, the ground control people can add to the general confusion by screaming commands at you every second or two. I think that instrument training is the great character building phase of aviation.

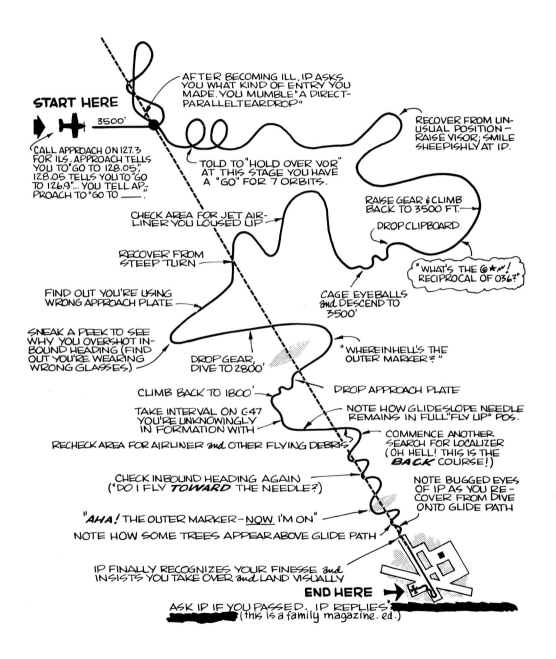

This story logically follows instrument training. If you're a pilot, you no doubt have noticed how controllers always manage to maintain a detached air in their discussions with you, especially when you're under the most trying circumstances. I'm told that air controllers face as much pressure as pilots—particularly in congested areas. I won't argue that point—but the farthest they can fall is off of their chairs to the floor. When you're mucking about up there in moderate-to-heavy turbulence with rain trying to drown out your engine(s) in a stacked holding pattern, comparison of tension is academic.

Most aviators in the metropolitan areas are over-controlled. They can receive instructions from no less than four or five controllers in transiting an area, say, of 40 miles. No sooner have you established who you're talking to and have changed the transponder code when you're asked to do it again—and again—and again. No wonder no one's looking out—pilots are slaves to their radio stack. I realize this is done to separate aircraft, but this business of constantly having your head in the cockpit runs 180 degrees out of phase with the purpose of "see and be seen" as a means of avoiding mid-air collisions. Of course, if you're buried deep in a nice cloud layer without much turbulence and very little other traffic around, having all that radar and those directions controllers give you is very, very comforting. As a matter of fact, I would much prefer to fly instruments in rather hairy weather than to fly across the Los Angeles basin on a crystal clear day.

There's always another side to the coin. F'instance, take the poor guy yo-yoing through the TCA in "moderate-to-unreal" turbulence—

Communications was once described as never having to say, "Huh?" It appears that there's some kind of contest between control towers and ground controllers to see who can talk the fastest and run the most words together. And as far as being intelligible, it's rumored that controllers are trained to talk with marbles in their mouths—when they've lost all of their marbles and still can't be understood, they graduate.

Pilots realize that there is a lot of chatter required in a controlled air space. But, in the long run, the machine-gun-delivery that one often receives from a controller just slows things down. Why? Because just about half way through your clearance or a new set of directions, the average pilot loses the continuity and from then on it's just plain playing catch-up. Once you get behind in your clearance, the rest of the clearance might as well be delivered in Sanskrit. When the tower or controller asks you if you wish any part of the clearance repeated, many pilots will say, "Yes, please repeat all after, 'ATC clears . . .'."

AND EVEN IF YOU TRY TO BE BRIEF—LIKE THE FAA ASKS—YOU CAN STILL RUN INTO TROUBLE ⸮

Readers often ask about where I get the names for locations and pilots appearing in my cartoons. Some of these sound suspiciously like real places and people. They are. Names like Fallbrick Air Park, Limbergh approach and Patmar Tower are thinly-disguised real airports near our home. Once in a while this can backfire, especially if I aim sarcastic barbs about personnel or equipment in their direction. Because our aircraft number—and particularly the paint job of our bird—is easily recognized I catch a lot of flak the next time around.

My first aircraft was a Bellanca Super Viking, the numbers of which I used in my cartoons. No sooner had this become pretty well-known in the local area than I decided to move up to a twin. I liked the anonymity this afforded. However, there was a hitch—the paint job. An ordinary paint job wouldn't do. We got a plane that was the most brilliant bilious yellow you could imagine—not just yellow in parts, but yellow all over. That's like trying to hide an elephant under a tea napkin. So whenever we appear on the scene and I've made a particularly caustic comment in one of my cartoons, I'll generally hear about it in cheap shots from either ground or air control.

If you've ever tried to find a dimly-lit air field near a well-lighted city then you can certainly sympathize with the poor joker in the last panel on the opposite page.

This episode is taken from Ching Willow's book, "Damn Serious Business." Ching is the nom de plume for a United Airlines pilot who, having been temporarily grounded, wrote a series of very funny articles and several books. He is a witty fellow with a great talent. One gets the distinct impression in reading this very funny book that it is the story of Ching's life.

The story opposite is allegedly fictional, but I believe it actually happened. Even in the early days when this episode transpired, O'Hare was a real zoo to get in and out of.

There's a happy footnote to Ching's story. At last writing, he had advised that he was back on flying status and now, in addition to writing funny material, he's flying the friendly skies.

WHEN JET AIRLINERS FIRST MADE THE SCENE SOME RATHER INTERESTING TRAFFIC CONTROL PROBLEMS AROSE

O'HARE TOWER THIS IS TIN GOOSE FLIGHT 2, IFR TO DES MOINES...

TRAINEE

ROGER TGA 2, CLEARED STANDARD IFR DEPARTURE. TAKE OFF RUNWAY 18, RIGHT TURN TO 270° CLIMB TO 5000 and MAINTAIN FOR 20 MILES BEFORE RESUMING OWN NAVIGATION...

HEY, RELIEF, TAKE OVER FOR A MINUTE WHILE I GO TO THE JOHN...

AS THE GOONIE LUMBERS OFF INTO THE OVERCAST, A BRAND NEW 707 WHEELS TOWARDS RUNWAY 18...

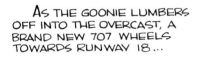

ROGER TRANSCON 12, USE STANDARD IFR DEPARTURE — AFTER TAKEOFF TURN TO 270°, 5000 FT. (ETC., ETC.,- SAME AS ABOVE)

AFTER THE 707 DEPARTS OUR SENIOR MAN RETURNS TO THE CAB

YOU RELEASED A 707 BEHIND THAT DC 3?!! OMIGOSH, THE CLOSURE SPEEDS! QUICK! MIKE!

TRANSCON 12 THIS IS O'HARE! REVERSE COURSE IMMEDIATELY REVERSE COURSE!

AFTER A BRIEF PAUSE, WE HEAR FROM GOOD OL' TGA,...

LOOK OUT, CHARLIE! HERE COMES THAT CRAZY S.O.B. BACK AGAIN!!

A couple more true stories on the opposite page. The tortoise and the aircraft was supposed to have happened somewhere in Florida, and I can believe it. You can find almost anything on the runways down there from alligators to cattle—particularly on some of the outlying air strips.

The notam was taken from the monthly update for Sky Prints. I can't imagine a more useless notam than to report a flock of geese, let's say over Nebraska, headed South. That notam will be valid just as long as the geese are headed South. The minute they turn West, hopefully there'll be another aircraft nearby to report this fact. We can't have uncontrolled geese flying about, willy-nilly.

The funniest notam story I've ever heard occurred at Edwards AFB, California. The Air Force closed the South Base and moved two very large hangars from that location to the North side of the new main East-West runways. These ponderous buildings were put on railroad flat cars, rail lines were laid across the new runway to the North side of the base and, in due course, a notam was issued. This notam, dispatched for the entire civilized world to read, read: "Edwards main base is closed due to hangars crossing the runway."

Aircraft salesman are a special breed. These are men who risk life and limb demonstrating aircraft to often-times unqualified pilots. The importance of making a sale, however, far outweighs the time and inconvenience it takes to check a man's credentials. When a salesman climbs into the right seat he usually does a lot of quiet praying.

These salesmen are not unlike their suede shoe brethren in the auto industry. Most of the time, you'll see them sitting around, feet on their desks, reading *TRADE A PLANE,* trying to conjure up some kind of a three or four way deal. But all in all, I tip my hat to these men because selling aircraft is not exactly like selling automobiles. There's often *long* dry spells between sales. Those dry spells occur irrespective of the cost of living—which, as everyone knows, has only one direction. One thing, *is* different from car sales, however, there's no putting sawdust in the transmissions to keep them quiet.

As a single engine rated pilot, your first impression of a twin's instrument panel is awesome. Not only are there two of everything, there are a lot more performance numbers to remember. And when a person goes into twin engine training, one soon hears such gibberish as V_{mc}, V_{yse}, V_{xse} and other seemingly undecipherable symbols. These are very critical speeds which have to be memorized and recalled instantly should one engine fail on takeoff.

On the subject of twin engine aircraft, many of the instruments have two needles on one dial, rather than two separate dials. Getting these needles lined up—or in "synch"—can be a nettlesome chore for the first couple of flights. I had one old boy tell me that the only time the two needles were in alignment with each other was when one was passing the other; one goin' up and the other comin' down. Finally, he came up to me and said, "I got it all figured out. Soon as I park the aircraft and shut down the engines, everything's in perfect alignment."

Pilots are real patsies for gagets aeronautical. The Lorelei call of a pilot's supply store is irresistible to a birdman. Perhaps worse are the mail order houses. Talk about wish books—an aircraft supply catalogue will beat a Sears catalogue any day in the airman's world. Buried in a vault back in Oklahoma City where the FAA records are kept, there must be a little man who gives out the names of pilots to catalogue printers. He's a very busy man because not a month goes by that three, four, or more catalogues enticing me to buy new equipment and gimmicks will find their way to the mail box.

Visiting a pilot's supply store can be a traumatic experience. Upon entering, you see the exact item that you've longed for for many months. After looking at the price tag (and picking yourself up off the floor), you ask, "Isn't there anything a little cheaper that does the job as well?" The answer is usually, "No." So what the heck, you go on a diet of dry cereal and burnt toast for a month and end up with that beautiful headset you always wanted.

Speaking about catalogues, the craze for computers seems undiminished. Those little circular cardboard or plastic discs that enable you to compute wind, ground speed, fuel consumption, etc., have now spawned a new generation of computers. Their offspring can tell you how to enter the 45 degree leg, what down wind leg heading should be, and what the horizon should look like on final. Next they'll tell you where to park. The circular jobs are giving way to those little imported hand held electronic brains . . . it boggles the mind! One of these days we'll be seeing a computer-of-the-month-club.

Speaking of the "horizon finder," I find it difficult to believe anyone who can pass a flight physical cannot find the horizon. One final shot on mail order: you can buy the entire aircraft that way providing, of course, the parts will fit inside your mail box.

Back to salesmen again. There usually isn't much high pressure salesmanship required in selling a bird to a dedicated aircraft buyer. The disease "buyitis" seems to strike an airman with unparalleled fury. People who impulse buy automobiles pale by comparison to a man with enough bucks in his pocket to buy an airplane and who is smitten by the flying bug. By the time he has looked at all of the aircraft that he has "had in mind" three or four times around, he usually homes in on one particular bird. That—and only that—airplane will be his. The problem comes in finding the man and the airplane and putting the two together There are just as many tire kickers in this field as there are in the automobile business. When you're selling, it's evident, right from the outset, when a man walks up to a machine you have on display as to whether or not he's a good bet. If he stands back for a minute or two and drinks it all in like a heady brew, he's pretty well hooked.

The cartoon on the solo flight was thrown in because it just seemed to fit here. There's nothing, just nothing, like your first solo hop in your OWN aircraft. That old adage about the two happiest days in a man's life are when he buys a "luxury" item—and again when he sells it only applies, in my experience, to the business of owning a boat. The parting of a man with his aircraft is a very emotional experience—unless, of course, he has just made a belly landing and is leaving because his continued presence would result in great bodily harm.

AVIATION GLOSSARY

LANDING FLAP: A 4000 FT LANDING ON A 3500 FT. STRIP.

"THE SOLO WENT FINE, NOW COULD YOU SEND SOMEONE OUT TO FIND ME?"

"IF YOU HAVE TO ASK SONNY, YOU CAN'T AFFORD IT"

The days of shaky non-scheduled airlines are pretty much a thing of the past—Federal Air Regulation 135 has seen to that. The requirements for flying charter operations now are almost as strict as the "heavy iron" carriers, e.g. the airlines. Does this mean an end to barnstorming? Probably.

Many of today's big carriers started out as non-scheduled airlines. But none of them made it to the top with lousy maintenance. Maintenance is something that many pilots, unfortunately take for granted. If you own an aircraft though, and make the required inspections, you certainly don't take it for granted. Not when you take a look at your bank balance each month.

The nonplused student pilot in the bottom panel is usually the the type that refers to an aircraft engine as a "motor."

ONCE UPON A TIME THERE WAS A NON-SKED WHICH HAD A NOTORIOUSLY LOUSY MAINTENANCE HISTORY...

THEN THERE WAS THE STUDENT PILOT WHO WAS SO DUMB (ALTOGETHER, NOW, READERS; "HOW DUMB *WAS* HE?") THAT WHEN TURNING ONTO FINAL and ENCOUNTERING A LARGE FLOCK OF BIRDS—
THE INSTRUCTOR SAID:

and HE SAID:

Computers again. Where would aviation be today without those little jewels? Back at Kitty Hawk, the makers of the computers say. We've got a full blown computer cult growing. Some aviators feel naked without a computer on their person.

The best computer ever devised is located in your skull between your ears. And when the unprogrammed happens, that computer can sort out the answers better than anything I've ever seen advertised in catalogues. The only trouble with the human brain is that it sometimes becomes overloaded and is unable to come up with a quick answer during times of stress. Take, for instance, the following scenario: You're in heavy weather, you're fighting to keep the aircraft straight and level, and you're flying a VOR course which bisects another VOR radial which forms a holding fix. Suddenly the ground controller tells you to take up a near-reciprocal heading and intersect another outbound leg of the first VOR—after reversing course you are to hold on a new radial of the second VOR. Quick! What's the answer?

Answer: Answer: Beats the hell out of me!

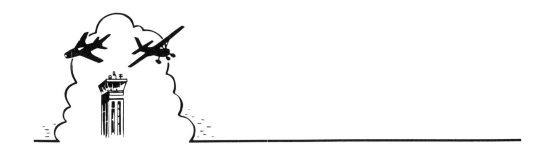

41

Here's a bunch of pot pourri plus some acronyms. And, again, communication. In the "It Never Fails" department, I'll never forget the first time I asked my mother to come and observe my landing at a field near our home. To appreciate this story, you'd have to know my mother . . . she is absolutely immobilized by fear of aircraft—particularly when she's in one. But I wanted to show her how safe everything was, and so I invited her out for a look-see. The results were disastrous. I think I counted four or five bounces before giving up on the first try and going around. The second attempt was not much better and finally in desperation on the third, I plowed through the weeds on the end of the runway rather than suffer the humiliation of another go-around. When I taxied back and jumped out to proudly display the fabric-covered little four banger to my mother, her only comment was, "Son, do you *always* land that way?"

In the tower sequence we have a little more of the FAA bureaucracy at work. I don't know why it's necessary to know how many souls are aboard an aircraft that is coming down like an anvil. But invariably somebody on the ground is going to ask that question when you're trying to make an emergency landing. The fact that you're coming down at an unplanned time and place sans part of the aircraft (that includes fuel) should warrant whatever ground equipment is available regardless of how many sweating souls are aboard.

"IT-NEVER-FAILS" DEPT:

YOU INVITE _____*_____ OUT TO SEE
YOUR PERFORMANCE AS A STUDENT
PILOT FOR THE FIRST TIME:

*6★!N-AN'
I BEEN GREASIN'
'EM ON FOR A
WEEK!

KASPRONG!

* CHOOSE ONE: YOUR FAMILY, GIRL
FRIEND, (BOYFRIEND?) LOAN OFFICER FROM
BANK, PROSPECTIVE PARTNER, ETC, ETC.

—AViATiON GLOSSARY—

MOA – A LARGE, EXTINCT, FLIGHTLESS BIRD
OF ZAMBOANGA THAT STOOD 12 FT TALL. ALSO
ACRONYM FOR MILITARY OPERATIONS AREA WHERE
YOU DON'T WANT TO BE WHEN THEY'RE
FIRING OFF GROUND-TO-AIR MISSILES!

RANCHO TOWER
THIS IS 34 VICTOR
I HAVE A FUEL
LEAK and RE-
QUEST ASSIST-
ANCE...

AIRCRAFT THAT
JUST CALLED RANCHO
TOWER, WHAT IS YOUR
TYPE ACFT, LOCATION,
NAME OF PILOT, PT. OF
DEPARTURE, NO. OF
PERSONS ON BOARD
— ETC.
ETC.
ETC.
ETC.

HOLD IT BUSTER!
HOLD IT! 34 VICTOR
HAS JUST BECOME
A GLIDER & I'M ABOUT
2 MORE QUESTIONS
AWAY FROM RAMMIN'
THE TOWER!

The central character in this little sketch is a crop duster pilot well known to those of us who fly in the Oceanside/Palomar/Fallbrook/Rancho California area. We'll just call him "Dusty." He's a real character of the seat-of-the-pants days of flying. He's got a great big old beefed-up Navy N-3N which lugs a ton or two. Dusty perches high atop an elevated seat where he can practically see the underside of his aircraft (a pretty important thing when you're flying a dusting operation).

Dusty rarely flies over 50 feet—I think he gets a nosebleed above that height. I tried to beat him on a short cross-country with my souped up Viking one day. At the departure point, Dusty poured the coal on and peeled off half way down the runway, disappeared around the corner of a hill and set sail for home. By the time I had taken off, cleaned up the airplane, set the proper mixture, manifold pressure and RPMs, Dusty had topped each ridge "with easy grace" of at least 50 feet, had made a straight-in approach and landed downwind on our home field. I had to set up a pattern and come in from the opposite direction. While the distance was not great and my speed advantage was on the order of 2 to 1, there was no contest at all. Which all goes to prove, I guess, that the race is not always to the swiftest.

This little montage points up some of the thrills of flying in the megapolis area between Los Angeles and San Diego. You may think that some of the scenes embellish the truth, but it is a fact that all of these activities take place—sometimes simultaneously—in an area a little over a hundred miles long by 30 miles wide. I was never quite so shocked as the day we came through the Cajon pass and heard a report of a hang glider at 6,000 feet on airways.

We are routinely routed around Lake Elsinore for parachutists jumping through cruising altitudes of 5-6,000 feet. Meantime, below and above the jumpers, gliders are soaring on the thermals rising from a nearby ridge. A few miles to the southwest, jets are pounding Camp Pendleton with high explosives, roaring to and from their home base at Miramar and El Toro, 50 miles away. Through all this B-52s from March AFB and airliners are shuttling about. (Several carriers have at least one plane per hour between the major cities in this area.) Add to this a covey of balloons and you have a real zoo!

The story about the old timer with the watery eyes comes from General Charles Yeager, one of our aviation greats. Chuck is an outstanding pilot and a great human being. Born in the hills of West Virginia, "so far up the holler they had to pipe in air," his dry wit has turned many a tight situation into a bearable one at Edwards Air Force Base where he test flew every conceivable type of aircraft. I've had the great honor to know Chuck during our service careers and have worked with him on projects since his retirement.

The oblique reference to the woman pilot is the only one you'll see in this book. It's not that I have anything against the gal flyers, it's just that I've heard very few humorous anecdotes about them (maybe it's because I don't attend their regular meetings., damn it!). The 99s, the women's premier flying organization in the U.S., has done a great job in supporting and furthering general aviation. These gals are real troopers and for some reason always seem to have more hustle in getting a race organized than their male counterparts.

The "What the Hell Do I Do Now" department was a more-or-less permanent feature I used in Air Force magazine. The situations apply to general aviation, also. Quite frequently while flying, you'll find yourself asking this question.

I got the idea for this cartoon from something which occured to me way back in WWII days. The whole story is too long for these pages—however, here's a short version: I was on a long, overwater flight in a P-51 when I tried to pull the relief tube from under the seat to perform a very important biological function. After much tugging and pulling the cup—and *only* the cup—came out and left the tube firmly clinched beneath the seat. That prompted an audible comment—"What the hell do I do now?". Quick as a flash, it came to me! I'll make a cartoon feature of this when I start drawing again after the War!

The story about the bush pilots isn't an exaggeration. Having flown with these folks—and in weather which would ground a seagull—the possibility of an aircraft colliding with a ferry boat in that part of the country is not unusual at all. I can recall recently flying around Vancouver Island with visibility of one-half mile or less and a ceiling of one to two hundred ragged feet. I commented to the pilot that I thought the weather was a bit sticky. His reply? "Nah, it's a pretty good day, actually. You should see it when it gets sloppy."

THE 'WHAT-THE-HELL-DO-I-DO-NOW?' DEPT.

YOU'RE APPROACHING THE INITIAL APPROACH FIX AFTER A BLADDER-BUSTING 3 HOURS OF SOLID INSTRUMENTS and FIGURE YOU CAN HOLD IT JUST LONG ENOUGH TO GET TO THE AIRPORT JOHN WHEN YOU HEAR:

(20 MIN. PAST THE HOUR)

AIR BANGER 8263 ROMEO, TRAFFIC DELAY. NOW EXPECT FINAL APPROACH CLEARANCE AT 44!

—AViATiON GLOSSARY—

CHOCKS: PIECES OF WOOD THE LINEBOY SLIPS IN FRONT OF THE WHEELS WHEN YOU'RE NOT LOOKING.

ROWR!

TRUE STORY. ALASKAN BUSH PILOTS HAVE BEEN KNOWN TO FLY IN SOME PRETTY SLOPPY WEATHER USING A PECULIAR IFR-VFR TECHNIQUE...(WHEN YOU CAN'T SEE AHEAD, LOOK OUT THE SIDE.) OUR SUBJECT IS CRUISING UP THE INLAND PASSAGE USING THE OL' "KEEP THE WINGTIP EQUIDISTANT FROM THE TREE LINE" BIT:

JEEZ, I HOPE THERE'S NO ONE COMIN' *DOWN* THE SOUND THIS WAY

CRUNCH!

VASHON

and, WHEN HE GOT BACK—

LOOKIT THAT, CLEM! I TELL YOU THEY AIN'T GOT NO RIGHT LETTIN' FERRY BOATS OPERATE IN WEATHER LIKE THIS!

TSK TSK

The building depicted in the upper right hand corner is taken from a photograph which adorns the wall at Flabob Airport in Riverside, California. You really have to see Flabob in order to appreciate this picture. Flabob is one of the last of the privately owned airports in the Southern California area. The airport is owned by Flavio Madariaga. This little strip, which has a 3200 foot asphalt runway (including some dirt overrun), sits cheek-to-jowel with busy Riverside Airport and is home for some of the most interesting aviation shops in the U.S. Hangars and shops ramble across acres—among them: Stitts Aircraft, Marquart Aviation, Antique Aero (with Jim Appleby's WWI masterpieces), Stol Starduster (with Flying Tiger ace Eric Shilling aboard), EEA Chapter 1, and a bunch of other people making specialized aircraft and equipment.

Debbie Gary, woman's aerobatic pilot, got her training at Flabob. A whole host of very famous aviators including the late Frank Tallman, have called this strip home. It's a marvelous place to visit and should become a shrine as the last bastion of private enterprise in the aviation sector. Drop in and say hello to Flavio. If you have strong constitution, try the hamburgers in the cafe.

I THOUGHT YOU SAID THIS WAS ONLY A *ONE*-HORSE AIRPORT!

(NO KIDDIN', FOLKS, THERE IS SUCH A PLACE!)

MAYDAY MAYDAY! I'VE LOST AN ENGINE *and* CAN'T MAINTAIN ALTITUDE! CLEAR THE PATTERN!!

ROGER, ROGER, AIRCRAFT CALLING PATMAR TOWER — WHAT IS YOUR POSITION?

I'M EXECUTIVE VICE PRESIDENT OF THE 1ST NATIONAL BANK! PLEASE EXPEDITE!

We've already mentioned Dusty so there's little else to be said about the cartoon in the upper left hand corner except that low flying aircraft will pick up some rather strange objects.

I remember being in a P-40 on a cross country training mission with a wingman in the southeastern part of the United States during WWII. We were tooling along at about 50 feet altitude when we decided to go down on the deck. There was a house up ahead and I radioed the wingman, "You take the right, I'll take the left." We went by just at prop tip level with the grass. When we returned to our home base, my wingman had picked up about 50 feet of clothes line which had wrapped around the pitot tube and he was hard pressed to explain how he could have possibly picked that up on a photo reconnaissance mission at 10,000 feet. One of the funniest sights I've ever seen is this young jock trying to cover that big wad of clothes line wrapped around the pitot tube with his leather jacket.

The bottom half of the page depicts something that confronts nearly every fixed base operator in the warmer resort and desert areas—the unannounced fly-in. "Sunday Fliers" will band together at the drop of a RPM and fly someplace. When they drop in, unannounced usually, they set upon the gas pump attendant, demand immediate servicing and then proceed to ravage the local cafe (which is probably geared to serve six hamburgers maximum per hour.)

The idea for this particular cartoon came as the result of a trip with a group from my hometown. We flew to a little place over in Imperial County near the desert. The cafe, however, was warned in advance and set up enough tables. We had a marvelous time. Fly-ins are a great way to get experience in cross-country navigation and still have a lot of fun and fellowship with other aviators.

A few more odds and ends. The "jugular vein" humor at the bottom of the page shows a situation most aviators have not been able to walk away from. But we can't always be serious in this business. The procedure of making a 180 degree turn upon entering instrument conditions as a non-instrument rated pilot has been taught for many years. It's an excellent way to extricate oneself from a sticky situation. Nine out of ten pilots who've had no instrument training won't last a nickle's worth of time in a cloud—particularly if they have to make a turn or two. There's nothing harder than a cumulus granitus.

The aviation glossary on gross weight reminds me of an ol' boy we used to call "Shakey" Trudeau. Shakey got his nickname from a bailout which was due, in part, to overloading. In this particular case, we were flying back from a trip to the East Coast in a couple of P-40s (the old Warhawk). Shakey had found a good buy in bourbon some place in South Carolina and had lightly strapped a case of "Ol' Rotgut" into the camera bay area on a rack behind the cockpit. The empennage control cables ran exposed through the fuselage right under the rack where the booze was perched. We got into some pretty hairy weather and apparently during one of the turbulent heave-hos, the case of bourbon slipped off the rack and landed on the elevator cables. This produced an immediate nose pitch-up condition. Old Shakey was startled and jabbed the stick forward. This apparently caused the case to leave the control cables and started ricocheting around the back of the airplane. Things happened rather quickly thereafter and Shakey found the airplane in a completely inverted and uncontrollable spin. He did the only prudent thing and bailed out. They found Shakey hanging in a tree by his parachute straps weeping copiously. When asked what the problem was, since he'd made it down safely, all he could say was, "Oh!_____there went all that booze." After this incident, Shakey shook so much it took two hands to get a glass from the bar to his lips.

One of the biggest air shows in the nation is the Confederate Air Force (CAF) AIRSHO blast every year in Harlingen, Texas— usually during the first weekend in October. This event draws pilots and observers from all over the United States, Canada and Mexico. It is a remarkable display of WWII aircraft and mock combat flying. In addition, some of the best aerobatic pilots in the nation perform. Their show is conducted every morning. In the afternoon, WWII is refought before your very eyes in authentic WWII aircraft fully restored and flown by CAF pilots. From the attack on Pearl Harbor right through to the dropping of the bomb on Hiroshima, you get the full seven course shot! I might add that the explosives used are the *real* stuff. (Except, of course, for the finale) Dynamite puts a real charge in things and when set off in front of the stands, usually results in several young ladies swooning away.

A tribute to CAF planning and expertise is the fact that there has not been a fatality to a CAF pilot or onlooker during the show in the many years it has been conducted. I've flown to the show in my own aircraft on several occasions and that in itself is a real experience. There's nothing quite like approaching an air field in Texas and suddenly finding yourself surrounded by Zeros and Messerschmitts. Hundreds of civilian aircraft crowd Rebel field in Harlingen. The overflow spills over to McAllen, Texas and a few other strips nearby. There just isn't enough real estate at Brownsville to park all the airplanes that come for this show.

Leaving the show is a real picnic. Try to visualize several hundred pilots all wanting to depart within about a 15-20 minute span of time. It resembles the 5 p.m. traffic onrush to the Los Angeles freeway. The tower at Harlingen struggles manfully with a myriad of requests coming from all sides. Usually, they'll give up and say, "Y'all get in line out there now, y' hear? And when you get to number one takeoff position give us your number. After takeoff, fly five miles straight ahead, take up a heading and go. Now y'all be careful, heah?"

You never know who you'll run into in the pattern at "Rebel Field"—

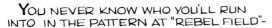

"Hey, Bob, I think this is the place..."

Participant pilots briefings were brief:

"Now y'all stay above 25 feet and don't do nuthin' dumb!"

The aerobatics that preceeded "the war" were SOMETHIN' ELSE!

"I wanna throw up but I don't know which way is up!"

Art Scholl in his Super Chipmunk doing the "Lomcovák"

Uniforms (silver grey, of course) make the man—

This is a Rebel aviator. If found lost or unconscious please hide him from Yankees. Revive him with a mint julip and assist him in returning to Southern Territory.

CAF Col (EVERYBODY's a col.) Tom Kelly...

Continuing with the Confederate Air Force show in Harlingen, the realism is so great that you actually find yourself wondering who's going to win. Japanese Zeros attack Flying Fortresses, Super Forts, and B-24 Liberators—P-40s, P-51s, P-38s, Wildcats and Hellcats mix it up with a wide assortment of Japanese dive bombers and torpedo planes. A crippled B-17 comes in on one wheel with an engine smoking. It really throws a chill up your spine to see all this happening right in front of you. I recall sitting next to the Mayor of Harlingen during one of the shows. He had to excuse himself for a few minutes to answer nature's call. Upon his return, the smoke was just clearing away from the final act and he turned to me and said, "Who won the war?"

I know all this sounds like a commercial for the CAF and it is. This outfit deserves a lot of credit. They are keeping alive the memory of those great machines and men who fought during WWII in all branches of the service. It's been costly in time, money and machines, but they've done a great job. The place is usually sold out. Hotels, with any kind of a room larger than a broom closet, and car rentals are sold out for months in advance of the show. Plan ahead and take your kids—you won't be sorry.

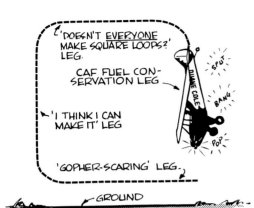

BEFORE THE "WAR" STARTED, DUANE COLE DID AN OUTSTANDING JOB OF SCARING HELL OUT OF EVERYONE...

and THE INCOMPARABLE BOB HOOVER DID A NUMBER IN A '51 CALLED "COLOR ME GONE."

THE "ACROJETS", BABY BEDE JETS FLOWN BY CORKY FORNOF and BOBBY BISHOP, LOOKED LIKE THEY WERE TIED TOGETHER.

THE WAR STARTED PROMPTLY AT 3PM EACH AFTERNOON. ONE DAY IT WAS D-DAY, THE NEXT, THE ATTACK ON PEARL HARBOR—

(P.S. IT WAS ALWAYS A THRILL TO FIND OUT WHO WON!)

This cartoon depicts the pre-takeoff briefing given to Rebel aviators at the 1966 Confederate Air Force show. The entire briefing, which was reprinted, is hilarious. It was dreamed up by that great humorist in the CAF ranks, Lloyd Nolan. Actually, the briefing and safety precautions are businesslike and detailed. The FAA is much in evidence and coordinate all activities with local authorities. There is a civilian side to the field and commercial airliners come and go during breaks in the show. All of the aircraft maneuvers, and we're talking about hundreds of sorties, are orchestrated very carefully through a net of air/ground communications.

The men who fly these marvelous WWII machines are, as everyone else in the CAF is, "Colonels" and, therefore, gentlemen. Even the ramp clean-up crew are "Colonels" (providing they've divvied up the proper amount of membership cash). There are the ladies, too, God bless 'em. Scores of gals make up the CAF ranks as members of the S.B.I. (Southern Bureau of Investigation) and other equally fascinating job descriptions. They all contribute time and money to see this thing work. Many Colonels have contributed tremendous amounts of money and time to restore these aircraft. If they are pilots, they are given a very careful checkout in all phases of the operation to insure against accidents. A bad one down there could ruin the whole show.

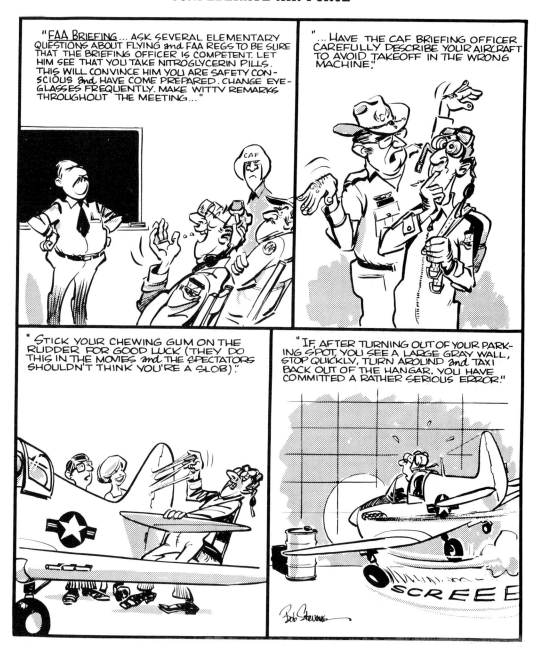

The quoted excerpts on the opposite page are actually taken from regulations "Concerning the Operation of Aircraft" as set forth by the United States Air Service in the year 1920. Actually, the comment on altimeters isn't very fair off. Even with today's sophisticated—and *costly*—instrument design, installation and checkout systems, my altimeter perversely decided to jump 200 feet the other day—the wrong way! Most instruments were very crude and rudimentary and altimeters were notorious for their lead and lag.

There have been military regulations concerning the use of "wing walkers" until the current time. It's not a bad idea for anybody moving around in a tightly-packed parking area. It's pretty hard on the brakes but it can save a nose-up or a wing tip. And I'll be darned if I know where the idea that pilots had to wear spurs came from.

"DON'T TAKE YOUR MACHINE INTO THE AIR UNLESS YOU ARE SATISFIED IT WILL FLY"

(OFFICIALLY, IT'S A "GARY FLYING MACHINE")

"DO NOT TRUST ALTITUDE INSTRUMENTS"

WELL, *MY* ALTIMETER SAYS WE'RE AT 5000 FEET!

"NO MACHINE MUST TAXI FASTER THAN A MAN CAN WALK"

"PILOTS WILL WEAR SPURS WHILE FLYING"

ACTUALLY, PARD, THEY MAKE OUTSTANDIN' BRAKES!

The carrying of a handkerchief was not a bad idea in the early days of open cockpit aircraft. The older engines that were used in those days had a propensity for throwing a lot of oil out through the exhaust stacks and rocker box covers. The handkerchief came in real handy for wiping off the windshield and one's goggles.

I guess the prohibition of riding on the parts of the aircraft was an attempt to stop greenhorns from trying to emulate the pros who were doing all kinds of far-out things like wing walking, hanging by their knees from the gear and jumping from ship to ship.

"If you see another machine, get out of its way" is one rule that is very basic to flying even today. The FAA has now relabeled this directive as "See and be seen." It is the biggest deterrent to mid-air collisions extant. We know from very dramatic events of the last few years that this very fundamental policy of keeping your head out of the cockpit and looking around "to avoid other machines" is very basic to keeping airplanes separated in flight . . . all the radars and controllers notwithstanding.

I'm sure that the order to land if an emergency occurred was not necessary in most cases those days because something either fell off the aircraft or the engine quit. But there are a surprising number of people who will press on with malfunctioning equipment, As an example, an acquaintance of mine who was (notice the use of tense here) an inveterate gambler was enroute to Vegas one time when he lost one of the two engines and started a long slow descent. Barely clearing the mountains, he squeaked into Nellis AFB. Jimmy the Greek won't cover odds on making that kind of a move. There's a four letter word that covers this type of operation and that's D-U-M-B.

"PILOTS SHOULD CARRY HANKERCHIEFS IN A HANDY POSITION TO WIPE OFF GOGGLES"

"RIDING ON THE STEPS, WINGS OR TAIL OF A MACHINE IN FLIGHT IS PROHIBITED"

"IF YOU SEE ANOTHER MACHINE NEAR YOU, GET OUT OF ITS WAY "

"IF AN EMERGENCY OCCURS WHILE FLYING, LAND AS SOON AS YOU CAN"

The gallows humor of the cartoon in the upper left hand corner carries a message: There *are* hazards and risks involved in flying—just as there are in other pursuits. This isn't a flying safety book, but we won't pass up an opportunity to "clean up our act." One of the biggest causes of accidents—as pointed out previously—is non-IFR rated pilots continuing flight into instrument conditions. And that's virtually a quote from the FAA statistic books. If just one cartoon can prevent somebody from practicing this type of Russian roulette, it's worth all of the books on flying safety rolled into one.

The delays in clearance depends on where you are and if you're in a computer line up. Almost everything is computerized these days, including instrument clearances. These computer centers are generally located a county or two away, in some cases a *state* or two. Once you have requested a flight plan and it is fed into the computer, the computer does not differentiate between one type of aircraft and any other. It merely puts them in order and, when your time comes up, you go. Los Angeles is an example of the computer running things (it *has* to—volume there's beyond human control). One of the problems is trying to get your request into the computer in the first place. It's virtually impossible to break into the line up because of the steady stream of outbound clearances tying up the frequencies. It's an absolute zoo!

Sometimes a VFR type clearance, which is necessary in a TCA (Terminal Control Area), will take up to 35 minutes in a place like Los Angeles. It's awful hard on engines and with fuel costs skyrocketing, hard on the pocketbook, too.

HERE'S AN OLDIE, BUT GOODIE –

No book of aviation humor would be complete without due notice of flight surgeons. Most of the pill rollers I knew in the service were gynecologists or pediatricians in peacetime practice. I've tried to connect those specialities with the doctoring of pilots but have failed to draw a parallel—unless it is the fact that pilots are upside down a lot and the docs are used to looking at folks that way.

Lady or baby doctors notwithstanding, the sawbones who give us our recurring medical exams seem to be a detached lot . . . to them, one body seems pretty much like the next. (I suppose I'd become calloused, too, after seeing all that meat and asking people to "cough—now once more" repeatedly.)

The reader may notice names of places or things in my cartoons. Usually, these are *real* names but, sometimes to protect the innocent, I'll disguise the label. In the case of Rancho California—shown opposite—it really *does* exist and is the field we call home. The wind howls across the strip (generally at 90 degrees to the prevailing runway) six months out of the year! It's no place for a novice in a tail dragger to practice touch-and-goes. There'll be more on Rancho California and its genial FBO, Jack Gallagher, later in this book.

(Incidentally, the poor mechanic watching the homebuilt come in looks a lot like Jack's side-kick mechanic, Chuck Helms, an ol' dope n' fabric troop from the great Tall-Mantz stable of mechanics).

PART II

We come now to military aviation humor and I might add since I put in 22 years with men in Air Force blue (and before that, "pinks and greens") the reader will note a strong leaning toward things Air Force. If this bothers you, just mentally substitute Navy, Marine, or Army aircraft and you'll not have a whit of trouble getting the most out of this section. Humor transcends mere machines and the color of uniforms.

Again we start with training since that always seems to be a logical place to begin. We move on to communications—again, the lack thereof making up the bulk of the genuinely funny stuff. There follows a series of cartoons dealing with operations and combat—known only to military aviators. If this turns you off, go back to Part I.

We round out things with a gaggle of events uniquely military which, naturally, would include such things as rules and regulations. Enjoy!

Many of our NATO allies took their early World War II training in the venerable Tiger Moth. These otherwise sturdy little birds had a penchant for shedding a wheel on takeoff—this, plus no radios aboard, made for some interesting stories.

The gentleman who sent me this idea is a Royal Netherlands Air Force fighter pilot, Martin Leeuwis. Martin is a very enterprising young man. He wrote to me about five years ago requesting permission to sell my books to overseas NATO air bases. He showed me a line of aircraft and pilot memorabilia which he was selling to fellow pilots. I immediately gave him permission. Since that day, he has sold hundreds of my books to various Dutch, German, French and Belgique airmen. He piles books and other memorabilia in the back of his jet fighter and sells them while tooling around Europe on training missions. Martin has several comic strips of his own; we're "birds of a feather . . ."

I have longed to own a Tiger Moth. It's such a simple and sturdy little machine. I literally drool at the sight of one. My bride is watching the checkbook closely these days—a friend of mine has a beautifully restored one on the market.

A<small>T A</small> RNAF (R<small>OYAL</small> N<small>ETHERLANDS</small> AF) T<small>RAINING</small> B<small>ASE</small>—

OH OH! THAT'S A STUDENT!! WE'VE GOT TO WARN HIM!

T<small>WO</small> I<small>NSTRUCTORS GRAB A SPARE</small> W<small>HEEL AND ANOTHER MOTI I TO GIVE</small> C<small>HASE.</small>

WE'LL HAVE TO SHOW HIM THE PROBLEM BEFORE HE TRIES TO LAND!

W<small>OULDN'T YA KNOW!</small> THE INSTRUCTORS' BIRD SHEDS A WHEEL UNBEKNOWNST TO THEM—

F<small>INALLY THEY CATCH THE STUDENT</small>—

HEY! THAT'S A NEAT TRICK! I WONDER HOWINTHEHELL THEY DO *THAT?*

 P.S. BOTH ACFT MADE REASONABLY *UNEVENTFUL* CRASH LANDINGS.

Stories like this tend to gain credibility when told and retold. As a matter of fact, one story which originated in one of my features many years ago came back to me in the form of a real life experience to a pilot in southeast Asia. I didn't have the heart to write back to the contributor and tell him that the idea he swore happened had, in reality, come from my imagination. (Y'know, it might have *actually* happened about the time I drew about it!) All this leads up to the fact that this T-6 blooper is supposed to have actually happened. I imagine both of the pilots involved made a silken descent.

This story also points up the blind, child-like faith cadets have in their instructors. I'm reminded of a young cadet in my class who was told that the aircraft we were flying at the time, the Ryan PT-22, aka "Maytag Messerschmitt,"had a propensity for throwing rods. The cadet was told that if the engine ever quit, particularly at night, he was to immediately bail out. Night forced landings in any kind of an aircraft is rather chancy business. One night the instructor thoroughly briefed our young man as follows, "If the engine quits and I point overboard, you *immediately* bail out!" It was a sparkling clear night and one could see for a hundred miles. The instructor, overcome with the beauty of the skies shouted to the student through a lousy Gosport (speaking tube), "My, isn't it a beautiful night!" The cadet had a short circuit between his ears and couldn't seem to get the message straight. He kept using a quizzical expression and cupping his hand over his ear. Remember now that the Gosport only transmitted one way, instructor pilot to student. Further, they were separated by a space of about three feet in their respective cockpits. Finally, in desperation, the instructor cut the throttle and pointed over the side to the lights below. He screamed at the top of his lungs, "Aren't the lights of Dos Palos pretty?" When he cut back the engine, the ol' Kinner that was propelling the PT-22 coughed, banged and sputtered. Response on the part of the cadet was immediate. He leaped over the side, pulled his ripcord and descended gracefully into the main part of town!

Taking a young newly-minted and often intimidated aviator and molding him into a roaring tiger of a fighter jock takes a lot of patience, practice and prudence. Ask any RTU instructor (who still has all his marbles).

This story was told to me by an air national guard pilot flying some of the latest equipment in the U.S. Air Force arsenal. These air guard pilots, or "weekend warriors" as they're sometimes derisively referred to, are a super bunch of combat-ready pilots. Eager, well-trained and ready to go, they fill the gap left by a skinnied down regular force. There's been a running street fight between the regulars and the reserve/air national guard as to the quality of pilots. Since World War II, we have depended more and more upon our air guard and reserves to bring units up to a combat readiness status. If there's any difference between the motivation and training of these groups, I can't find it—they're all ready.

Don't let the cute dialogue—ala first grade primer—turn you away from this funny true story. (Cartoonists have fits of being cute at times and this one just slipped out.)

Kenny Gereaux, a World War II ace, told me this story about another ace friend of his, Dick West. One day during advanced training, Dick was out making touch and go landings away from the main base. The retractable landing gear was new in advanced trainers at that time. This innovation and controllable pitch props gave neophyte birdmen a whole bunch of trouble in the early days. There were frequent belly landings. Commanders' efficiency ratings often hung in the balance of how many belly landings their charges would make in a given period of time. Strict orders were handed down and court martials were not uncommon for this type of inattentiveness on the part of the pilots.

There's a story of one cadet who landed gear up and flipped over on his back. Looking around, he noticed no one was watching his particular area of the field at the time and he pumped the gear into a locked position while upside down. (Note: He didn't get away with it.) West got away with his scam.

FLY, DICK, FLY. SEE DICK FLY. SEE DICK MAKING LANDINGS AT AN AUX. FIELD. SEE DICK LAND GEAR UP!

@*!☼⚡ NOW I'VE BOUGHT A WASHOUT RIDE FOR SURE!

SCREEE

SEE DICK LOOK AROUND. LOOK, DICK, LOOK. HEAR DICK'S THOUGHT WHEELS TURNING. THINK, DICK, THINK!...AHA!

HMMM-- NOBODY OUT HERE.

HEAR DICK MAKING A RADIO CALL. CALL, DICK, CALL. HEAR MAIN BASE PANIC. PANIC, MAIN BASE, PANIC!

TOWER, THIS IS CADET WEST. I'VE LOST MY ENGINE ABOUT 20 MILES SOUTH OF THE MAIN BASE. INSTRUCTIONS, *PLEASE*

DON'T PANIC WEST! ESTABLISH NORMAL GLIDE! TRY TO MAKE *ANY* FIELD! KEEP COOL! CRASH CREW'S READY, ETC., ETC., **ETC.**

WATCH THE LARGE HAND MOVE 5 MARKS ON THE WATCH, ER, CLOCK ?

HEAR DICK SAVE HIS GLUTEUS MAXIMUS. GOOD SHOW, DICK, GOOD SHOW!

TOWER, THIS IS CADET WEST. I COULDN'T MAKE THE MAIN BASE, BUT MANAGED A BELLY LANDING AT AUX #2!

OUTSTANDING JOB, WEST! CONGRATS!

Here we have a little bit of training in various stages of the flying career of a cadet. Advanced training is shown in the case of the poor instructor pilot who just led his first practice formation flight. Basic jet aerobatics were taught in the venerable T-33—not a real barn burner when going straight up.

There's also a number on navigator training, which is conducted, in part, in the T-37 Cessna "tweety bird" or "converter" (it converts fuel into noise). The other shot depicts a hotshot jock of a superfort instructor pilot, ready to go on a long mission in the old B-50 aluminum overcast.

Back to the ol' T-bird or T-33; it was an honest machine but it sure didn't like to fly backwards. It had a nasty habit of slipping tail first out of a vertical stall. It bitterly resented this particular method of flying—as any self respecting aircraft would. I got into such a maneuver one time with a young crew chief riding as observer in the rear seat. After a snappy vertical roll of several turns, I ran out of air speed and started to rapidly lose altitude rearward. Sure enough, the old T-bird snapped over and went into about three turns of a spin upside down before I could get it into a right side up spin (which is hairy enough). Finally, I recovered and pulled out about 5,000 feet above the ground. I was flying straight and level waiting for my pulse rate to return to somewhat near normal, when I heard the Sgt. pipe up from the rear seat, "Gee, Major, that was a NEAT maneuver! Do that one again."

LET'S LOOK AT A TYPICAL "SUPERFORT" INSTRUCTOR PILOT DURING THE POSTWAR ERA.

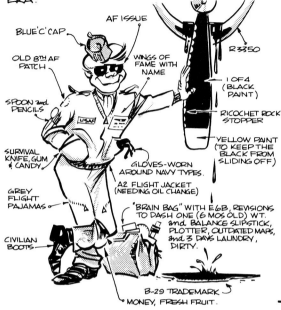

BLUE 'C' CAP

AF ISSUE

OLD 8TH AF PATCH

WINGS OF FAME WITH NAME

SPOON and PENCILS

R 3350

1 OF 4 (BLACK PAINT)

RICOCHET ROCK STOPPER

YELLOW PAINT (TO KEEP THE BLACK FROM SLIDING OFF)

SURVIVAL KNIFE, GUM & CANDY

GLOVES-WORN AROUND NAVY TYPES.

A2 FLIGHT JACKET (NEEDING OIL CHANGE)

GREY FLIGHT PAJAMAS

"BRAIN BAG" WITH E6B, REVISIONS TO DASH ONE (6 MOS OLD) WT. and BALANCE SLIPSTICK, PLOTTER, OUTDATED MAPS, and 3 DAYS LAUNDRY, DIRTY.

CIVILIAN BOOTS

B-29 TRADEMARK

MONEY, FRESH FRUIT.

NAVIGATOR TRAINEES APPROACH RIDE FM-5 (AEROBATIC FAMILIARZATION IN THE FIGHTER ENVIRONMENT) WITH ZEST and ENTHUSIASM! PICK OUT THE STUDENT WHO JUST HAD A LUNCH OF TACOS, BEANS, FOOT-LONG HOT DOG and FRIES—

BAG, BARF

T-37

THE T-BIRD DIDN'T HAVE THE THRUST-TO-WEIGHT OF AN F-15...

THEY, THEY, THEY TRIED TO KILL ME...

...LED HIS FIRST CADET FORMATION PRACTICE FLIGHT...

YAS! BUNIONHEAD! WHEN THE AIRSPEED READS "0" AND THE SMOKE FROM THE TAILPIPE BLOWS BACK PAST THE CANOPY, WE'RE *NOT* GOIN' ANY HIGHER!

USAF

This story came from a Chinese National Air Cargo ex-Flying Tiger pilot. It's a true story about a C-46 driver and a check pilot in the early days of CNAC's history flying cargo around the Asian continent. The ol' "Commando" was a sturdy bird, but it sure as hell didn't like to fly sideways.

Multi-engine drivers pride themselves on how quickly they can detect and "clean-up" a dead engine. Just remember that the aircraft wants to turn into the dead engine and you'll keep this story straight (which is more than can be said about the aircraft after it finished this maneuver).

CBI (CHINA-BURMA-INDIA) CHECK RIDE IN AN OL' C-46

THEN, BEFORE THE ENGINE QUITS, THE CHECK PILOT STOMPS ON THE **LEFT** RUDDER!

THE CHECKEE STOMPS ON THE **RIGHT** RUDDER TO KEEP DIRECTIONAL CONTROL JUST AS THE MILL QUITS and...

QUICKLY FEATHERS THE **LEFT** PROP!

We now leave the carefree, devil-may-care days of training and enter the operational unit. Don't be dismayed by the depiction of prop and jet jobs on the same page. We leap over the span of three wars in less than the margin width on this page and others.

Communications is still an underlying theme on the pages that follow. It just seems that if anything can foul up on the RT (Limey for radio-transmitter), it will.

In the lower right hand corner, the case of two aircraft diving on the same target happened to many pilots during WW II, Korea and Viet Nam. It seemed there just weren't enough enemy aircraft to go around at times. A quick way to get the man ahead of you out of the way for a nice clean shot was to yell, "Break! Break!" This would immediately divert the man ahead of you (and everybody else on the same frequency). This little ploy wasn't recommended for cementing relations between leaders and their wing men. If you pulled it once too often you were liable to find yourself in a cargo outfit or lugging VIPs around the back waters of the war in a liaison-type aircraft.

WAY BACK IN '56, A FLIGHT OF DUTCH F-84F's* LAUNCHES INTO A LOW OVERCAST. A 2ND SECTION PULLS ONTO THE ACTIVE FOR RUNUP-

PULL IT UP, HENK!

(F/O HENK)

2ND SECTION

* WHICH HAD A PROPENSITY FOR BLOWING UP.

JUST BEFORE BRAKE RELEASE, NO.2 IN THE SECOND SECTION - A PILOT NAMED HANK- HAS PROBLEMS.

HANK! GET OUT!! YOU'RE ON FIRE!

COMMON FREQ

BAROOM!

GUESS WHAT HAPPENED, FOLKS? YER RIGHT, HENK BAILED OUT!

?

P.S. HIS ACFT FLEW AROUND - PILOTLESS- FOR ABOUT 10 MIN. BEFORE AUGERING IN!

AND ONE SURE WAY TO UP YOUR SCORE and LOWER YOUR POPULARITY- WAS TO HOLLER "BREAK!" WHEN YOU and SOME OTHER GUY WERE AFTER THE SAME TARGET,...

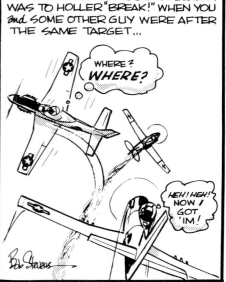

WHERE? WHERE?

HEH! HEH! NOW I GOT 'IM!

Bob Stevens

This has to be the ultimate in foul-ups in communication. I'm indebted to the *TALON*—official cadet newspaper of the Air Force Academy—for this hilarious scenario. Only minds strained to the breaking point by undergraduate study could come up with a libretto like this one.

The cadet authors of this remarkable sequence are wise beyond their years because this is the way it really *is* and ever shall be no matter what branch of the service we're talking about. I wonder what the Gettysburg address would have looked like after being passed through 3 or 4 echelons?

Tomorrow evening at approximately 2000 hours, Halley's Comet will be visible in this area, an event which occurs only once every 75 years. Have the men fall out in the flight line area in fatigues, and I will explain this rare phenomenon to them. In case of rain, we will not be able to see anything, so assemble the men in the theater and I will show them films of it.

By order of the Colonel, tomorrow at 2000 hours, Halley's Comet will appear above the flight line area. If it rains, fall the men out in fatigues, then march to the theater where this rare phenomenon will take place, something which occurs only once every 75 years.

By order of the Colonel in fatigues at 2000 hours tomorrow evening, the phenomenal Halley's Comet will appear in the theater. In case of rain in the flight line area, the Colonel will give another order, something which occurs every 75 years.

Tomorrow at 2000 hours, the Colonel will appear in the theater with Halley's Comet, something which happens every 75 years. If it rains, the Colonel will order the comet into the fight line area.

When it rains tomorrow at 2000 hours, the phenomenal 75-year-old General Halley, accompanied by the Colonel will drive his Comet through the flight line area in fatigues.

One of the things that could numb an old military air transport pilot with terror was to "get violated" by penetrating the air defense identification zone (ADIZ) at the wrong spot. Fighters policed this line, which runs completely around the United States, and would turn you in at the drop of a nautical mile.

I suppose it's no secret to readers by now that I flew fighters. Quite frankly, I delighted in bouncing aircraft that strayed into "no-no" areas. The sheer speed differential between the bouncer and the bouncee was enough to strike terror into the hearts of the staunchest of airmen. Transport and bomber crews were especially sensitive to high speed passes directly in front of their windshield. Having unidentified aircraft tooling around in areas that are extremely sensitive to our national security is something that the United States frowns upon. Our instructions were to intercept offending aircraft straying into the wrong airspace and then make a hard turn in front of the offender to indicate the direction he should turn (most of the time we did not have direct radio contact with the aircaft involved).

I remember catching an American Airlines DC-6 right over the middle of the White Sands restricted area one day and throwing an F-86 across the bow of the airliner at some 600 miles per hour. The DC-6 immediately followed our instructions, but not before ground controllers had picked up his foul. I understand the unfortunate captain of that trip was fined severely and grounded six months. An incident like this could prompt a "near miss" report. Near misses are just that—and scary as hell. I'll never forget the sign tacked on the men's room wall at one base which stated: "Pilots will report all near misses!" And down underneath, written in crayon by some latrine artist, was the following addendum: "After you've changed your drawers, of course."

Between the wars (any two since World War I will do), airfields normally saturated with traffic while the shooting was going on, tended to fade into obscurity. This story is about just such a place and was told to me by a Flying Tiger captain who's had some marvelous exchanges with towers worldwide. His stories of attempts to communicate with him in broken English would make a fabulous book by itself.

Around every controlled airport in the United States and abroad, there is a five mile circle into which you should not fly without first contacting the tower and getting permission. I have heard pilots call for landing instructions almost on top of the field. If the tower operator wants to be difficult, he can send the aircraft back out to the five mile limit to reenter in the proper manner. This is carrying the rule too far, particularly in these days of high cost fuel. There would be fewer of these arbitrary hijinks if the tower operator had to share the extra fuel bill with the redirected pilot. End of sermon.

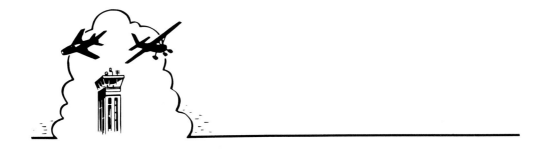

KARACHI TOWER, THIS IS MATS NINER FIVE TWO, TEN MILES OUT. TRAFFIC ADVISORY, PLEASE.

ROGER, OLD CHAP. YOU'RE CLEARED TO RUNWAY 27 — AS FAR AS TRAFFIC GOES, WE 'AVEN'T 'AD *any* BLOODY AIRCRAFT 'ERE SINCE LAST TUESDAY — SHE'S ALL YOURS.

OUR PILOT, A PERSISTENT TYPE, MAKES SEVERAL MORE TRAFFIC PATTERN CALLS

KARACHI, FIVE TWO TURNING DOWNWIND. ANY REPORTED TRAFFIC?

I REPEAT! NO TRAFFIC. THERE 'ASN'T BEEN A SOUL 'ERE SINCE *LAST TUESDAY!*

SUDDENLY:

KARACHI TOWER, WHADAYA MEAN SINCE LAST TUESDAY? THERE'S A GUY COMIN' *RIGHT* AT US OFF RUNWAY OH-NINE *NOW!*

OH, DEAR, I *DO* 'OPE WE'RE NOT GOING TO 'AVE ANOTHER DAY LIKE LAST TUESDAY...

"Silence is golden" according to an early Swiss inscription. Silence is also *mandatory* in Air Force formations from home base to the target (the enemy had ears, too). This is an old tale and it *could* have happened—and near Swiss territory, for that matter.

Communications at certain times are absolutely essential to maintain one's sanity. A little levity can break the teeth-grinding pre-combat strain of flying a bomber stream to the target. However, our leaders, being leaders, had to be serious. Once you reached the bomb line there was supposed to be absolute silence on the radio. If you were in trouble, that was another story.

One of the most famous songs to come out of World War II was a story about a young fighter pilot surrounded by enemy aircraft down on the deck somewhere near a railroad station. His radio call went like this: "Help! Help! I'm being clobbered." His leader, high above in the security of six miles altitude asked, "Where?" Whereupon the young pilot replied, "Down here on the railroad track." Hence, the old song which went, "Help, help, help, I'm being clobbered—down here on the railroad track . . ." The words are sung to the tune "Tromp, Tromp, Tromp, the Boys are Marching." (Try singing it—it has a certain lilt.)

We now move into the operational training and combat arena. The P-38 was particularly vulnerable to zany ideas for new missions and armament because its size, speed, and tremendous load-carrying capability.

Did you ever think, "Who in the hell came up with *that* idea?". Usually it was some bushy brain in old five sides by the Potomac. Many times, however, these strokes of genius came from misguided souls in our midst—even down to the squadron level.

The tail warning radar rang a bell, which sounded like a cheap alarm clock. And it went off right next to your ear. It was guaranteed to straighten out your hair and mark your linen in a helluva hurry.

A checkout ride stuffed in the back of an early P-38 used in training (officially, it was a RP-322) was an experience to be forgotten. As the checkee, you were crammed in a hot, sweaty, little compartment with parachute partially strapped on. In this grotesque position, you were expected to observe everything that went on over the pilot's shoulder. Usually, you ended up heaving all over his back before the first loop was completed. I know. I was on the receiving end on several checkout rides. I learned to take along a barf bag for the checkee.

P-38 development went on until they actually made a bomber out of one, complete with bombardier's compartment in the nose. We had P-38s dropping bombs all over the place with the lead P-38 bombardier locked in that sweaty nose compartment. The poor soul had no method of escape should any harm befall the bird.

SCREWBALL IDEAS WE'D LIKE TO FORGET!

A POX ON THE GENIUS WHO EXCHANGED THE DROP TANK BUTTON ON THE CONTROL WHEEL FOR THE MIKE SWITCH

WE'D LIKE TO CATCH THE CLOWN WHO—IN THOSE EARLY & ELECTRONICALLY UNSOPHISTICATED DAYS—THOUGHT TAIL WARNING RADAR WOULD BE A GOOD THING ON FIGHTERS—

AND A FURLINED BARF BAG TO THE IDIOT WHO THOUGHT A CHECK-OUT RIDE SHOULD CONSIST OF STUFFING YOU INTO THE RADIO COMPARTMENT WHERE ALL YOU COULD SEE WAS THE PILOT'S NECK & ALL YOU SMELLED WAS 100/130 OCTANE—

MAY THE GUY WHO THOUGHT OF USING DROP TANKS AS PERSONNEL CARRIERS BE CONDEMNED TO RIDE THROUGH THE HEREAFTER IN ONE—

The night fighters' lot was a lonely one—solitary birds stalking their prey in pitch black conditions. Pilot and radio operator (RO) were an inseparable team both in the air and on the ground—*usually.* At the height of Air Defense Command's heyday, this event actually happened. If you've ever been awakened in the dead of night by a wailing claxon, you can understand how.

I tried to be a night fighter pilot while in advanced flying training and talked two of my closest buddies into applying for this special assignment. I wanted to fly the Douglas A-20 attack bomber which had been painted black, armed with many machine guns and cannons in the nose and called a P-70 for night fighter work. To make a long story short, my two buddies were able to pass the night vision test, which was a much more rigorous test than the mere 20/20 vision required for day fighter pilot qualifications. I flunked. My buddies went on to lead very colorful careers in the night fighter ranks.

All flight and ground personnel were glad these night fighter chaps were about. It's the only way we could get a decent night's rest in a combat zone. These night stalkers kept the enemy's harassing "washing machine Charlies" away so we could get our much-needed sleep.

This page is strictly a polyglot with an emphasis on feet—yes, feet! In war, be it on the ground or in the air, the saying "Take care of your feet and they'll take care of you" applies. Here again you see the venerable P-38. It was drafty in that nose compartment and they never did get a heater that would keep you warm below the kneecaps.

I had a couple of hundred hours in this bird and came to respect and admire it for its toughness. After you'd lost an engine and had to come several hundred miles back on one fan, your admiration grew in leaps and bounds. But the P-51, which you also see depicted here—and on other pages—was my favorite. It was a true fighter pilot's aircraft. The designer, one Ed Schmud, of North American, was an old Dutchman who knew how to design airplanes (he had worked for Anthony Fokker of Germany—which was good basic training). It is rumored that Ed sat a pilot in a chair and drew the lines of the P-51 around his subject. You literally wore a P-51. It was slick, fast, maneuverable and had long legs for escort duty. The bomber boys dearly loved the '51 when they made those long-range raids against Berlin.

As a final note, a great tribute was paid to the P-51 by its enemies. Both the Germans and Japanese feared it as our deadliest fighter.

IN THE P-38, ILL-FITTING NOSE COWLING (AROUND THE GUN PORTS) PRODUCED A SUB-ZERO CONDITION AT THE RUDDER PEDALS...

...WHILE IN THE P-51, STRADDLING THAT MONSTROUS V1710 ALLISON BROUGHT THE COCKPIT TEMP UP TO THAT OF BOILING WATER *

PORTRAIT OF A NOVICE PASSENGER WHO MISTOOK THE EARPLUG WAX HANDED OUT FOR A PIECE OF CHEWING GUM ?

THERE ARE FEW MEN STILL FLYING WHO RODE IN THE BEHEMOTH B-36D. THOSE WHO DID MAY REMEMBER THIS CLASSIC EXCHANGE BETWEEN AN IP & A PILOT ABOARD ONE OF THE *10* ENGINED AERIAL TITANS:

Let's take a look at our English cousins during "the big one." They had a vocabulary of flight that was unique and as far removed from ours as the United States was from jolly old. Pilot Officer Prune is our equivalent of Roger Rudder—a young, dashing fighter pilot.

The Australians also had a very unique vocabulary of *their* own. Most of it was unprintable. A classic story about an Australian and the radio-telephone involves a United States pilot who was checking his microphone. The Yank, who obviously had left his headset unplugged, was blowing into the microphone at regular intervals requesting, "How do you read me, how do you read me? Testing, one, two, three, four, one, two, three, four." These transmissions went on at intervals for approximately 30 minutes and, of course, he could not hear a reply. Note: His broadcast was being transmitted over some five hundred square miles of ocean in the Western Pacific. Finally, an Australian pilot flying in the area piped up with, "Al'right, mate, ya've been blowin' in me ear now for 'alf an hour, when are ya going to kiss me?"

The Hurricane shown on the opposite page shot down more German aircraft than its well-known counterpart, the Spitfire, in the Battle of Britain. Fortunately, before this terrible period in 1940, the British manufactured a great number of these marvelous "Hurries." They were part fabric and part metal. It was acknowledged by the Hawker-Siddeley group that, if the aircraft had been produced initially with a larger engine, it probably would have been able to handle the entire air supremacy chore for the British.

These stories were told to me by General Chuck Yeager. Many readers will recall that General Yeager was the first man to break the speed of sound back in the "good old days," 1947. He achieved this remarkable feat in the X-1, "Glamorous Glennis," a rocket ship which now hangs in the Smithsonian Institution. General Yeager is retired now but still flies Mach 1 plus aircraft. He punches through sound with a NASA bird every year on the anniversary of his historic flight.

General Yeager is a real practical joker. Some of his stories about the early days of Muroc Air Base, later to become Edwards AFB, and the fun the test pilots had both on and off duty (particularly the times at Pancho Barnes' "Happy Bottom Riding Club") would make a great book.

In the early days of jet aircraft, these propellerless machines were viewed as apparitions from another world and struck downright terror in the hearts of some transient ground crewmen. Pilots, not unmindful of this effect, were prone to take certain advantages. I suspect that in both of these stories, General Yeager played a prominent role.

"If God had intended man to fly, he would have given him wings"—so goes an old saw which we might amend to: "If God had intended man to fly *instruments*, he would have also given him a built-in artificial horizon." Weather has always been held in awe by most airmen. It can be benign or awesome. The trouble is that a pilot rarely knows when it's going from benign to awesome when he's in the soup. If you're boring along and all of a sudden things get black and bumpy, you often wonder "what the hell am I doing up here?"

A pilot has to depend on a lot of people on the ground plus his own considerable skills to get through bad weather and safely back on the ground. It's small solace to hear a man in a nice warm room some two or three miles below say "radar shows no heavy weather in your area" while you're slopping through ice, snow and freezing rain. However, those folks on the ground—the controllers, GCA men, and tower operators—can often mean the difference between life and death. Weather forecasters are another breed of cat, however, and some of the stuff they hand out is pure fabrication.

Weather forecasting is certainly not an exact science; it may not even be a *science*. To prove my point, one time I stopped at Hill Field, Utah and after a detailed, lengthy technical briefing by the weather forecaster, I finally asked him if it was clear enough to get through the mountains to the East. The man laid down his pencil, walked to the window, opened it, stuck his head out and looked to the East. Then returned to me and said, "Yeah, it's clear."

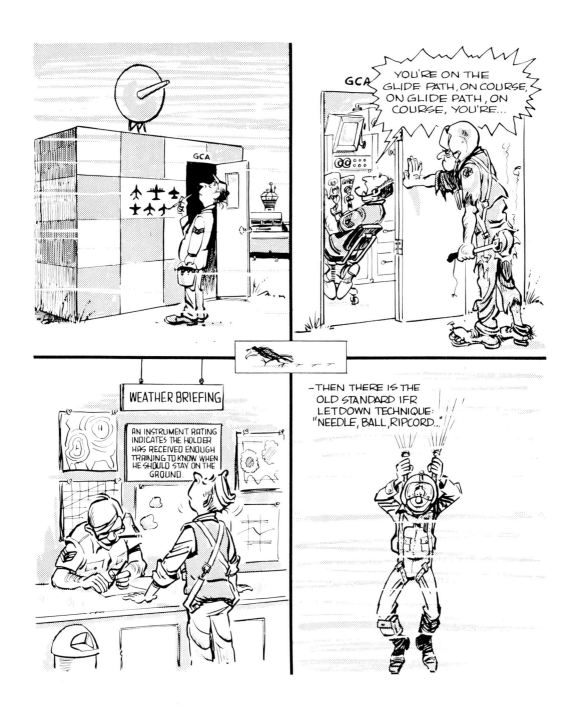

Let's stroll down the memory lane of aircraft microphones. I wish I could say, like the cigarette commercial, "You've come a long way, baby," but I really can't.

Microphones and radio/telephone procedure are often misused. Pilots have an almost compulsive tendency to break the boredom of a long flight by talking on the radio. Recalling the earlier case of the Australian, there was the case of another pilot who kept blowing into his microphone, "Testing, one, two, three, four. Testing, one, two, three, four. Testing, one, two, three, four" over and over again. He was driving everyone in the area mad. Finally, he requested the tower to give him a reading. The tower replied, "You're coming in two by two" which is a code for readability and signal strength. The pilot shot back, "What's two by two?" Then some other joker in the area came back with, "You're comin' in *too* damn loud and *too* damn often!"

There have been many funny instances regarding microphones and trainees. There was the cadet who reported once to Merced tower on the downwind leg with this call, "Hello, Merced tower. This is cadet Dumbjohn in aircraft 1234. Give me landing instructions, please, I've lost my headset." Then there was the case of the cadet who was switched to intercom by his instructor in the rear seat. When the cadet called the tower for taxi instructions, the instructor—camouflaging his voice to sound like the tower—told him to stand up in the cockpit so he could be seen because the tower was unable to identify the aircraft. Sure enough, the cadet rolled back the canopy and stood up and very sheepishly looked around.

SOME SADIST DESIGNED A THROAT MIKE THAT WAS SUPPOSED TO FREE YOUR HANDS (BUT TO KEEP FROM CHOKING, YOU HAD TO LEAVE IT LOOSE & HOLD IT TO TALK ANYWAY).

I SAY AGAIN... AWK!

ZZZAP

(P.S. SWEAT "SHORTED 'EM OUT" and LEFT BURN MARKS ON YOUR NECK)

BRITISH WWII MODELS WERE IN A FABRIC FLAP WITH THE OXY MASK. THE PROTRUDING EARPHONES CAPPED THE PICTURE.

I SAY, YANK, LET'S GIVE 'ER A RUDDY GO!

THEN THERE WERE THE CUMBERSOME HANDHELD JOBS. GREAT WHEN ALONE, TRYING TO MAKE AN IFR APPROACH, LAP FULL OF MAPS, 3 GUYS TALKIN' AT YA, ETC., ETC.

WHERE IS THAT DAMN THING?

FINALLY, WE PROGRESSED TO THE LIGHTWEIGHT LIP MIKE—WHICH YOU CAN ALWAYS EAT IN TENSE SITUATIONS —

WE JUST LOST NO. 4, TOO?

ULP!

NOTHING, BUT NOTHING, EVER BEAT THE HUMAN VOICE BOX WHEN IN A REAL JAM—

WHICH WAY TO IRELAND?

LINDBERGH IN "SPIRIT OF ST. LOUIS"; N.Y. TO PARIS, 1927.

We've had an exchange pilot program between the armed services for many years. This story involves an Air Force blue suiter operating Navy machinery off the coast of Viet Nam. The plane is a "SPAD," or Skyraider. There was also an Air Force version of the Skyraider, or AD-1.

I do not begrudge the Navy pilots one iota of the comfort they enjoy aboard carriers. When you stop to think that they must take off from a moving air field—and a very short one at that—find an enemy out over trackless miles of water, come back—perhaps with battle damage—and try to land on a postage stamp heaving in a rough sea, they deserve all of the creature comforts that man can muster.

It always kind of bugged us Army and Air Force types, though, that when we were down to the bottom of the barrel as far as food and beverage was concerned, we would have to go beg from the Navy. There they laid offshore in their big, gray vessels crammed to the gunnels with food and booze.

AN AD-5 SKYRAIDER (AKA THE "SPAD") IS ON A CARRIER'S CATAPULT READY TO LAUNCH WITH A TRUCK LOAD OF STORES.

MEANS: "MY INSURANCE'S PAID UP, I THINK I'M READY TO GO."

A BROKEN CATAPULT YOKE - JUST A MINOR MALFUNCTION - LEAVES THE SPAD IN PLACE BUT CATCHES THE WOUND-UP PROP...

... and FLINGS THE R-3350 A COUPLE OF MILES OUT TO SEA ➡

MEANS: "ON SECOND THOUGHT, CAN'T WE TALK THIS OVER?"

No book on aviation humor would be complete without at least a page or two of "famous last words"—such utterances as: "Where in hell are we? I'm the navigator, I've got a right to know!" or, "That engine sound rough? Nah, it's just blowin' its nose, pull the gear up!" or, "Nah, those are friendly fighters," or, "If I can just track him another second or two, I'll have 'im," (while an enemy aircraft is boring in on your tail). Another famous last utterance is, "What makes you think I can't fly under that bridge?" We could go on and on, but I'm sure you get the idea.

The non-rated officer at the Viet Nam fighter base bar must have some kind of a death wish because, if there's one thing fighter pilots will fight to the last man for, it's to protect the Jolly Green Giants. These brave helicopter crews picked up over 2,000 downed airmen from the jungles of Viet Nam. The story of the Jolly Greens is one of extreme heroism. There should be a book about them if there isn't already.

FAMOUS LAST WORDS

During World War II, the AAF issued wings for just about any job that involved an aircraft. There were just about as many types of wings as there were jobs on the flight line. There was one common element about the issuance of wings to personnel—you had to fly in order to get a pair. To the girls we were trying to impress, it didn't mater much what was depicted in the center of the wings just as long as we had those nice, shiny hero badges. With these on your chest, doors were opened, drinks were poured and dances freely given.

In looking over the variety of wings, it occurred to us that we might superimpose in the center of the wings an item that would best describe the job the wing-wearer held. For the non-AF readers, the words "stand board" refer to a standardization board which was really a flight check crew. They went around and made flight crews' lives miserable by giving them air and ground checks—sometimes in the middle of the night.

116

JUST SUPPOSE THEY DECIDED TO MAKE THE WINGS REFLECT THE JOB?

NEWLY-MINTED COPILOT

AIR LIFTER

STAND BOARD

HELICOPTER

FIGHTER PILOT

HEADQUARTERS

On the next couple of pages we cover the Thunderbirds. This magnificent aerobatic air-borne drill team started out as the Acrojets back in the late '40s flying P-80 jets. They've progressed steadily over the years to hotter and hotter flying machines. They currently fly the T-38 supersonic advanced trainer, the "Talon."

The Thunderbird's counterparts in the Navy are called the Blue Angels and their drill is equally impressive. In order to keep this cartoon in its proper perspective, remember the story about the old farmer who saw his first barnstorming aircraft and said, "I see it, but there ain't no such thing!"

Not too long ago I was offered a ride in the number four "slot" aircraft of the Thunderbird team. They were practicing near their home base at Nellis Air Force Base, Nevada. I don't know how I got out of the deal, but I was glad I did. The ol' boy they stuck in the rear seat in my place, came down with a cracked helmet. It seems the slot pilot, "Fig" Newton, forgot to tell his passenger that he was going to do the Bon Ton Roulle, which is a high speed snap. You've got to hunker your head down on your neck in order to keep it from flying off. As Fig went into the roll, the passenger's head whip-lashed and hit the side of the canopy. All during the debriefing this poor chap's eyeballs kept going around until he finally got 'em caged.

TAKE OUR SUBJECT, FOR EXAMPLE—
HE'S SEEING HIS FIRST DEMONSTRATION
BY THE USAF THUNDERBIRDS ...

FORMATION ROLL
ON TAKEOFF

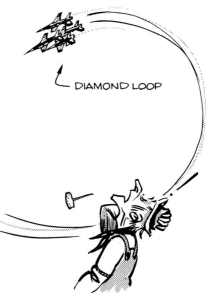

DIAMOND LOOP

FOR ALL WHO HAVE SEEN THESE
LADS PERFORM—YOU KNOW HOW
TIGHTLY THEY HANG IN THERE...

BON TON ROULLE

UNTIL THAT FINAL "BOMB BURST"

BY CRACKY!
I *KNEW* IF THEY
KEPT FOOLIN' AROUND
WITH THAT DERN
THING, THEY'D PULL
IT APART!

119

To all who have seen our nation's outstanding air demonstration teams perform, one thing is very apparent—their absolute precision in everything they do. Now this precision business can be carried too far.

My wife, Barbara, came up with this gem while we were watching the Confederate Air Show in Harlingen, Texas. All she had to say to me after the mission was over and the fellows were marching off the ramp was, "I wonder if they go to the bathroom that way, too?" That was enough to set off this sequence.

Postscript: The leader of the team told me this cartoon was actually in error—only the leader has a zipper in his flight suit, they want to keep the rest of the team humble.

The story on the top of the opposite page was told to me by a night fighter pilot named Dick Ehlert from Fort Walton, Florida. We laughed over this one while at a reunion of World War II night fighters in Colorado Springs several years ago. All of which brings up one of the methods I use to get cartoon ideas. I spend quite a few weekends per year traveling around and visiting World War II unit reunions. Additionally, I fly to active duty bases and get into hangar flying sessions with the local jocks. One overnight trip to an air base with a chance to belly up to the bar and talk to the lads can provide enough material for several months of cartoons. If there's one thing a pilot— particularly a fighter pilot—likes to do, it's drink and tell stories.

Then, too, I have some pen pals who like to share humorous anecdotes they've heard or experienced with others. Some ideas are unusable because they can't be "sanitized" sufficiently, others because they are not graphically feasible, e.g., how do you draw 1001 fighters in one sector of the sky and 1000 in another with someone in the former group saying, "C'mon, let's jump 'em—we've got 'em outnumbered!"

TRUE STORY: TOWER HAD TO REPEAT WARNING INSTRUCTIONS RE 200' TREES 800' OFF END OF ONE RUNWAY; THE INEVITABLE HAPPENED–

BLAZER 28, WISH TO ADVISE THERE ARE **800 FT.** TREES 200 FT. OFF APPROACH END OF RUNWAY... CLEARED TO LAND.

ROGER, TOWER, ON THE 800 FT. TREES! HOW *THICK* ARE THEY?

THEN THERE WAS THE MOTHER WHO VISITED HER SON'S WW II OUTFIT *and* WASN'T OVERLY IMPRESSED BY THE NOSE ART.

NITE TAKEOFF

"WELL, IT'S ALL VERY NICE, SONNY, BUT I DIDN'T NOTICE ANY PICTURES OF THE PILOT'S *MOTHERS* UP THERE!"

WHAT KINDA MANUEVER YOU TRYIN' TO PULL, MR?

ME? I THOUGHT YOU HAD IT!!

Fighter pilots, being fighter pilots, are wont to engage in aerobatics at the drop of a bomb to impress their brethren in the bigger iron birds. The "big friends" have a few impressive maneuvers of their own.

This episode reminds me of a little maneuver I pulled late in World War II which almost cost me an airplane. Coming back to Okinawa from a sortie to Japan, my wing man and I happened to cross a lone B-29 straggling towards Okinawa. We were bored by the long flight and decided to liven up the party by making a dive and a roll in front of our lumbering big friend. At the top of my roll over the big bird, I got my feet and hand coordination crossed up and came out of the maneuver in a violent side slip. Now this is well and good if you're down to pattern speed, but if you're doing 400 plus, it's liable to tear you apart. Fortunately, the airplane was a strong one—the P-51. I snapped out of it with a couple of blooper rolls and went into a gorgeous flat spin, recovering some two or three hundred feet above the water. My wing man said, "Gee, that was a nifty maneuver. I'll bet you impressed the hell out of 'em with *that*!" And there's no telling what the people inside the B-29 were saying.

DURING THE MOST RECENT UNPLEASANTNESS, F-4s ESCORTING B-52s WOULD OFTEN DO AILERON ROLLS AROUND THEIR CHARGES—

FINALLY, ONE OL' '52 COMMANDER COULD STAND IT NO LONGER—

LOOKIT THAT CLOWN SHOWIN' OFF!

LISSEN, LIL' FRIEND, I CAN DO SOMETHING YOU CAN'T... WATCH!

THERE! I'LL BET YOU CAN'T DO *THAT!*

I DIDN'T SEE ANYTHIN'— WHATJA DO?

I JUST SHUT DOWN **TWO** ENGINES —*and* I'M WAITIN' FOR YOU TO TOP THAT!

Once upon a time there were NCO pilots—"flying sergeants." They flew anything that had wings and was painted olive drab. As more second lieutenants were minted, the sergeants were relegated to what has been referred to as "garbage" flying, e.g., slow timing engines, ferrying, towing targets and flying liaison missions.

When this cartoon first appeared, I drew some flak from a local pilot & A and E who was to later become a friend. This fine gent's name is Jack Gallager and he's the FBO at a Southern California airport near our home. Jack was an ex-flying sergeant who was stationed in Burma flying with the First Air Commandos. He flew in some very hair-raising combat situations—evacuating wounded, spotting artillery and generally assisting the allied effort. He took great umbrage at the term "garbage flying" and set me straight on *that* count in a hurry. His photographs of the job these flying sergeants did in the God-forsaken jungles of southeast Asia made me eat those "garbage" words.

Some of these sergeants were made Flight Officers, which is an air-borne Warrant Officer. We called them "blue pickles" because of the insignia they wore on their shirt collars. Most of these Flight Officers were later given commissions as second lieutenants en masse. Some of 'em didn't like it because, as Warrant Officers and flying sergeants, they were authorized free uniforms and chow. When they became commissioned, they had to eat in "open" messes (if you could have seen some of the shelter halfs we used for mess halls, you would understand where the term "open" mess came from) and *pay* for that mess.

TWO OL' CAJUN-TYPE 3 STRIPERS ARE
PROPPING AN L-4 "GRASSHOPPER" (MR. PIPER'S
CUB IN O.D.)

HENRI GETS "CAUGHT UP"
IN HIS WORK—

THE CONTINENTAL 4 BANGER HITS ABOUT
5 LICKS BEFORE JACQUES CAN CUT THE
SWITCHES—

127

"*Communicate*—v.t. 1 To give to another . . .impart; transmit." Webster doesn't say anything about *receiving* and that, dear readers, is the subject of this cartoon. Thomas Fuller, the famous author said it all in, "Birds are entangled by their feet and men by their tongues."

Here we are back to the ubiquitous communications again. When you run out of breathing oxygen at altitude you suffer from a malaise known as anoxia or hypoxia. One of the symptoms is extreme euphoria. It's a strictly "no sweat" situation— that is until everything goes to hell in a hand basket.

Incidentally, the P-70 depicted is the aircraft I mentioned earlier that I wanted to fly upon entering the service. I had worked at Douglas Aircraft on this particular type of aircraft and thought it was one of the finest machines around. It served as a stop-gap fighter until true radar carrying night fighters could be developed. Actually, it was a good light bomber but lacked a lot of the things that night fighter pilots needed, the least of which was speed.

1943 - A P-70 * IS OVER GUADALCANAL CHASING THE ELUSIVE "WASHING MACHINE CHARLIE" AT ANGELS 20 - OXYGEN IS RUNNING LOW...

HEY, BUDDY, WE AIN'T HAD A LIL' OL' VECTOR FROM GROUN' CONTROL "KIWI" FER A LONG TIME *

RADAR OPERATOR

ROGER, OL' TROOP. MUSH BE TH' RADIO ANTENNA'S SHOT AGIN... WE BETTER PANCAKE *

H'LO KIWI. THIS ISH RED ONE. OUR ANTENNA ISH BROKEN and WE CAN'T TRANSHMIT. OVER.

* LAND

* NIGHT-FIGHTER VERSION OF DOUGLAS A-20 HAVOC.

ROGER, RED ONE. UNDERSTAND YOU ARE UNABLE TO TRANSMIT. RETURN TO BASE and PANCAKE.

ROGER, KIWI.

* SHOUNDS REASHONABLE T'ME... *

OR HOW ABOUT THIS NEWER GEM ?:

AIR FORCE ONE NINER FIVER HOLDING AT TWO ZERO THOUSAND, I CAN EXPEDITE YOUR APPROACH IF YOU CAN DESCEND TO TWO THOUSAND IN TWO MINUTES.

NO SWEAT, APPROACH, CAN DO - BUT I WON'T HAVE NO AIRPLANE WITH ME WHEN I GET THERE!

Now it can be revealed—the real nomenclature of a World War II fighter! We provide you aircraft historians this phantom cut-away drawing showing the intricacies of a typical warbird. These are the official terms of the Confederate Air Force which, they report, have been stolen from only the most authentic publications.

Again we run across material from that bastion of World War II aircraft and memorabilia, the Confederate Air Force. The CAF has produced a glossary of aircraft terms which is one of the most hilarious documents I've ever read. Unfortunately, about 70% of it would have to be sanitized for use in a book of this type, which we consider to be PG rated—at best.

CUTAWAY – WW II FIGHTER (OURS)

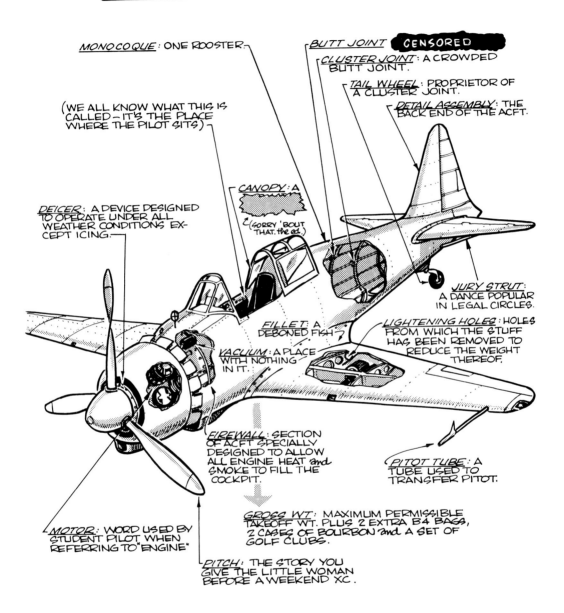

MONOCOQUE: ONE ROOSTER.

BUTT JOINT ▬CENSORED▬

CLUSTER JOINT: A CROWDED BUTT JOINT.

TAIL WHEEL: PROPRIETOR OF A CLUSTER JOINT.

DETAIL ASSEMBLY: THE BACK END OF THE ACFT.

(WE ALL KNOW WHAT THIS IS CALLED – IT'S THE PLACE WHERE THE PILOT SITS)

DEICER: A DEVICE DESIGNED TO OPERATE UNDER ALL WEATHER CONDITIONS EXCEPT ICING.

CANOPY: A ▨▨▨▨ (SORRY 'BOUT THAT. the ed.)

JURY STRUT: A DANCE POPULAR IN LEGAL CIRCLES.

FILLET: A DEBONED FISH.

LIGHTENING HOLES: HOLES FROM WHICH THE STUFF HAS BEEN REMOVED TO REDUCE THE WEIGHT THEREOF.

VACUUM: A PLACE WITH NOTHING IN IT.

FIREWALL: SECTION OF ACFT SPECIALLY DESIGNED TO ALLOW ALL ENGINE HEAT and SMOKE TO FILL THE COCKPIT.

PITOT TUBE: A TUBE USED TO TRANSFER PITOT.

MOTOR: WORD USED BY STUDENT PILOT WHEN REFERRING TO "ENGINE"

GROSS WT: MAXIMUM PERMISSIBLE TAKEOFF WT. PLUS 2 EXTRA B4 BAGS, 2 CASES OF BOURBON and A SET OF GOLF CLUBS.

PITCH: THE STORY YOU GIVE THE LITTLE WOMAN BEFORE A WEEKEND XC.

Great air battles were often fought in officer club bars among crewmen. Most such battles were won—and a few were lost.

After publishing this cartoon, I found out there *really* was a P-400. It was a variant of the P-39. I was told that there weren't too many of them built and they were mostly used in the South Pacific. Of course, the guy who came up with the gag didn't know about this either and when I used the material, I got letters from no less than ten or so P-400 pilots.

Close scrutiny of your work is something that all artists and cartoonists must expect. There are World War II history buffs who count guns, rivets and what have you of every plane drawn. They know the nomenclature of any aircraft or piece of equipment used and you'd better label 'em right or you'll hear about it. The barrage balloon story is one case in point. Backed by what I thought to be an unimpeachable source, I called barrage balloons in one cartoon "anti-aircraft" balloons because the cables hanging therefrom were intended to sever the wings of low flying German aircraft in the Battle of Britain. I had no sooner released the drawing than graduates of barrage balloon schools started writing to me, sending certificates and all kinds of records to prove that there was no such thing as an anti-aircraft balloon. I found out that anything which was suspended in the air from which you observed or which you used to knock down enemy aircraft, carried the title of barrage balloon. I swore off balloons forever after that one.

THEN THERE WAS THE QUEASY NON-RATED MAJOR RIDING IN THE BACK OF A B-25 WHO WAS TOLD BY A CREWMAN:

Scenes like this raise the "pucker factor" to its zenith and make a feller a trifle edgy. (The co-pilot just caught his sleeve in the throttle quadrant as a cannon shell burst in the cockpit and has been screaming, "I'm paralyzed!") This B-17 happening has been widely reprinted—mainly on the covers of reunion programs of World War II bomb groups. The markings are of the 91st Bomb Group, which was stationed at Bassingbourne, England. The surviving members of this famous Group have made me an honorary member, of which I am justifiably proud.

To show that we're not plying favorites, we put a B-24 sequence in just below the B-17. The 24, also known as the Liberator, was the other big load carrier in the air force's inventory during World War II. The episode depicted points up the axiom, "There are no atheists in foxholes." This saying applied equally to men in air combat as well as ground forces. As a matter of fact, I doubt you'd find an atheist on the far side of the bomb line in *any* war.

In ANOTHER CASE A '24 HAS ITS HAT *and* HANDS FULL—ONLY THIS BIG BIRD HAS A CHAPLAIN RIDING IN THE NOSE SECTION—

It's about time we recognized those unsung heroes of EC (stands for Electronic Counter measures). The old "humpback" AKA EC-121 super Connie, or "swineicus subsonicus" as referred to by her crews, has been doing a super job for several decades. But there is one thing about the old girl—she's slow. As a matter of fact, pilots who wrote songs about her in the southeast Asian theatre of war often referred to her as the "Lockheed flying speedbrake."

Most of the gear aboard was highly classified electronics gear. She carried a large crew of scope scanners. It was alleged the 121 was so slow that most of the crews got in their complete combat tours just flying out to the patrol area and back on one mission.

IN SEA, 121s FLEW _DEEP_ INTO UNFRIENDLY AIRSPACE ON BUTT-NUMBING MISSIONS. PROTECTION CONSISTED MOSTLY OF SIDE ARMS _and_ (ALLEGEDLY) THE FOLLOWING IN-FLIGHT TACTIC:

WE GOT A MIG LOCKED ON US!

AT THIS DISQUIETING BIT OF NEWS, THE PILOT WOULD OPEN THOSE FOUR OL' R-3350-93 ENGINES WIDE...

R0AR!

65 GALLONS OF CRUDDY OIL PER ENGINE EMITTED

WELL, SIR, THAT OIL WOULD COMPLETELY DRENCH THE TRAILING ENEMY...

SPLOOSH! ?

HE'D EITHER ① OPEN THE CANOPY, LOSE HIS MASK _and_ PASS OUT, OR ② FLAME OUT FROM SUCKING IN ALL THAT OIL!

SCRATCH ANOTHER, CAPT.!

HEH! HEH! THAT'S 4 THIS MONTH!

BLUB!

P.S. IF THIS DIDN'T GET HIM, A FULL BLAST OF RADAR WOULD RENDER HIM IMPOTENT _and_ HE'D DIE OF "LOSS OF FACE" UPON RETURN TO HIS BASE!

Here we have bail-out stories from several wars—or somewhere in between. These are all allegedly true and, as we all know, truth is funnier than fiction.

No story about bail-outs would be complete without the case of the crewman on an AT-11, which was the advanced navigator trainer built by Beech Aircraft. She was also known as the C-45. It seems that on a night cross country, this particular AT-11 ran into some very heavy weather and the crew was advised to bail out. The plane was loaded with navigator trainees and everyone started pushing to get out the door. The crew chief got into line without his parachute being completely tightened up. When he got to the door, he was shoved out by the man behind him while his 'chute was still hanging limp on his back. He managed to hang onto the edge of the door and crawl back in while trainees plummeted past him. By the time he got back in and the chute was on, the worst of the weather was over and the pilot elected to land with this very shaken troop in the rear. The story goes that from that time on, the chief would never board the aircraft without first putting on his parachute. Upon landing he would get out of the plane, stand on the ground, take off his chute and put it back in the airplane.

OUR FIRST SUBJECT—A C-46 CREW CHIEF
NAMED DON BUSSART—COULD SLEEP ANY-
WHERE—ANYTIME. PARKED ON THE RAMP,
HE'S SAWIN' LOGS WHILE ANOTHER BIRD
RUNS UP ON THE NEXT PAD...

THE NEIGHBOR SHUTS DOWN—

SINCE WE'RE ON CONDITIONED REFLEXES,
WWII CREWS GOT *THE WORD* EARLY ON—

LISSEN! IF I SAY 'BAIL-OUT' DON'T COME BACK WITH 'WHAT DID YOU SAY?' BECAUSE YOU'LL BE TALKIN' TO YOURSELF!

INSTRUCTORS ARE INSTRUCTORS
TO THE END—EVEN WHEN THEY FOR-
GET THEIR SEAT BELTS...

YA **STILL** CAN'T DO A DECENT, SLOW ROLL!

Most of our AAF World War II fighters, with the notable exception of the P-47 and P-61, were powered by liquid-cooled, in-line engines. (If you think I'm going to get into the pros and cons of this decision, you're crazy.) There was one thing for sure about the in-line engines, however, when you were out of coolant—you were out of luck.

Air-cooled engines were less vulnerable to ground fire since there was less plumbing exposed. On the other hand, the large radials had a frontal flat plate area that created extra drag. The in-line more streamlined liquid-cooled engines had a propensity for popping their coolant at very critical times—like right after takeoff on a hot day or when perforated by a small hit in a coolant line deep in enemy territory. A liquid-cooled engine sans coolant will run very few minutes before seizing up solid like one big block of metal. When those long 16 cylinder babies froze, the inertia of four 12 foot propellers stopping in a half turn or so could flip you on your back. Whew! I get the clanks just thinkin' about it!

WHEN VARIOUS FIGHTER GROUPS MIXED IT UP WITH THE ENEMY OVER THE BOMBER STREAM—and ALL ON A COMMON FREQUENCY—MISTAKES WERE BOUND TO HAPPEN...

HELP! I'M HIT and LOSING COOL-ANT! WHAT'LL I DO?

CALM DOWN AN' FEATHER IT, BUDDY!

FEATHER IT, HELL! I'M IN A MUSTANG!

ONE WAY TO DETERMINE WHETHER THE PUDDLE UNDER YOUR BIRD WAS FUEL OR COOLANT—A MIXTURE OF ALCOHOL and WATER—WAS TO DIP A PINKIE IN and TASTE IT.

PORTRAIT OF A PILOT WITH A LEAKY COOLANT TANK

— ME WORRY?

This one's hard to believe but the guy it happened to—Jim Crocker, Oklahoma State Director of the Combat Pilots Association—has the scars (and the medals) to prove it. Jim has kept this little episode more or less a secret over many years for obvious reasons.

Jim's tour as a called-up national guard cavalryman serving in Africa and Sicily resulted in his being perforated several times. While convalescing in the United States, he figured out there's got to be a better way to fight a war than on the ground so he transferred to the AAF. After getting his wings, he went back into combat as a P-51 pilot. Returned home again, he ferried P-51s to the Russians in Alaska. The way he got back into combat a *third* time was unusual. He was ordered to Alaska one time and he and his wingman decided to go to Houston instead. They became "disoriented" and tried to stay in that Texas city for the duration. When finally located, he received swift movement overseas and another combat tour. Jim wound up the war with a chest full of medals, including six purple hearts, one of which he obtained in the episode depicted here.

LATE IN WWII, THE AAF'S 9TH TAC IS SUPPORTING THE 90TH INF. IN PUSHING THE RETREATING GERMANS HARD UP AGAINST THE CZECH BORDER –

HOT DAMN! SCRATCH 4! BUT I'M OUTTA ROCKETS. IF I CAN JUST HERD THAT LAST TANK OVER THE HILL, THE BAZOOKA BOYS 'LL GET HIM.

THE STRICKEN PZKW RAISES ITS 88-mm TURRET GUN and SQUEEZES OFF A DESPERATION SHOT AT CROCKER, THE GADFLY.

KA POW!

BY PURE CHANCE A TANK CANNON ROUND HAS HIT AN AIRPLANE!

GEEZ! A THING LIKE THIS COULD RUIN YOUR WHOLE DAY!

BLOOIE!

JIM BELLIES IN – A CZECH GIRL PULLS HIM FROM THE WRECK and HIDES HIM...

LOOKIT THAT! and HERE I AM – OUTTA COMMISSION

...IN A CELLAR STOCKED WITH BRANDY! TEN DAYS LATER THE U.S. 4TH ARMORED LIBERATES THE PLACE –

RESCUE? WHO N' HELL WANSA BE RESCUED? HIC HIC